EDITING RENAISSANCE DRAMATIC TEXTS

Conference on Editorial Problems

Previous Conference Publications

The Conference volume for 1976 will deal with medieval texts and will be edited by A.G. Rigg.

Copies of all previous volumes are available through Garland Publishing, Inc.

EDITING RENAISSANCE DRAMATIC TEXTS ENGLISH, ITALIAN, AND SPANISH

Papers given at the eleventh annual
Conference on Editorial Problems,
University of Toronto,
31 October-1 November 1975

EDITED BY ANNE LANCASHIRE

Garland Publishing, Inc., New York & London

1976

Library of Congress Cataloging in Publication Data

Conference on Editorial Problems, 11th, University
    of Toronto, 1975.
    Editing Renaissance dramatic texts, English,
Italian, and Spanish.

    Includes bibliographical references and index.
    1. Editing--Congresses. 2. Drama--15th and
16th centuries--Congresses. 3. Drama--17th century
--Congresses. I. Lancashire, Anne Begor. II. Ti-
tle.
PN162.C62 1975   808'.02   76-7324
ISBN 0-8240-2410-9

To the home team

Contents

Notes on Contributors

BEATRICE CORRIGAN is Professor Emeritus of Italian at the University of Toronto, and has recently edited two Italian Renaissance plays for Manchester University Press. She is Co-ordinating Editor of *The Collected Works of Erasmus* (University of Toronto Press) and a member of the Editorial Committee of *Renaissance Drama.*

G. BLAKEMORE EVANS, Cabot Professor of English Literature at Harvard University, is Textual Editor of the 1974 Riverside edition of Shakespeare's works. His past editorial work has generally focused on Shakespeare; and he is especially to be thanked for his on-going *Shakespearean Prompt-Books of the Seventeenth Century* (5 volumes to date).

ARTHUR FREEMAN, until mid-1975 with the English Department at Boston University, has now moved to London, England, as an independent scholar and poet. Author of *Thomas Kyd: Facts and Problems,* and editor of reprint series of Renaissance texts, he is currently at work on a new edition of Kyd's works.

G.R. PROUDFOOT is General Editor of the Malone Society and a Lecturer in English at King's College, University of London. His recent publications include an edition for the Malone Society of John Heywood's *Johan Johan*; and he has collaborated on the Malone Society texts of *A Yorkshire Tragedy* and the forthcoming *Faithful Friends* and *The Wasp.* Also editor of *Two Noble Kinsmen* for the Regents Renaissance Drama Series, he is presently at work on a new edition of *The Shakespeare Apocrypha.*

ARNOLD G. REICHENBERGER, Professor Emeritus of Romance Languages (Spanish) at the University of Pennsylvania and a member of the Hispanic Society of America, was co-editor of the *Hispanic Review* until his retirement in 1973. He has recently edited (with Augusta E. Foley) Lope de Vega's *El primero Benavides,* and has just completed a catalogue of the dramatic manuscripts of the Spanish Golden Age in the library of the Hispanic Society of America.

EDITING RENAISSANCE DRAMATIC TEXTS

INTRODUCTION

Anne Lancashire

The papers included in this volume were presented on 31 October and 1 November 1975, on the University of Toronto campus, at the eleventh annual Conference on Editorial Problems. Within the general topic of editorial problems the Conference deals each year with a different field; in 1975 Renaissance dramatic texts took their turn as the focus of papers and discussion. Three different literature areas — English, Italian, and Spanish — were specifically represented; and although it was a pity that the traditional length of the Conference, and the practical necessity of emphasis on one language, did not allow other literatures such as French to be the subjects of papers, other literatures were by no means neglected. As always, the problems discussed were largely ones of interest to editors whatever their particular literature or language, and also to bibliographers, press editors, and special-collection librarians. The delegates to the Conference came from a variety of areas and academic disciplines, and from across both Canada and the United States. Informal discussion among delegates — facilitated by distribution at the Conference of a list of those in attendance, with their current research interests noted — was of major importance in the success of the event. Unfortunately such discussion cannot be represented in the Conference volume.

As was inevitable, papers and conversation alike, at this eleventh Conference, turned to the two questions basic to most human endeavour, including editing: what has been done so far in the area of particular concern to us? and in what directions should we now move? The editing of Renaissance dramatic texts has been most vigorously pursued, in this century, in the field of English literature: in which, as G.R. Proudfoot writes, "more [editors] must be alive at this moment than at any previous time." It would perhaps have been thought, then, that a look at the past by English Renaissance editors would have produced a reaction quite different from that experienced by Italian and Spanish editors looking back in their own special fields. Surprisingly, however, all five speakers agreed, although for different reasons, that the accomplishments of the past — both distant and immediate — left much to be desired. In Italian and Spanish Renaissance drama, past editorial practices have often been lax, and some major texts have yet to appear in modern editions. In the field of English Renaissance drama, the names of a few twentieth-century editors and bibliographers — Greg, McKerrow, Hinman, Bowers — evoke instant respect and the belief, at first, that all basic principles have been established and that little must remain to be done other than walking with the lesser-known texts of the period along a clear path towards the attainable goal of good standard editions of most extant plays. At close view, however, the situation seems very different. G.R. Proudfoot, G. Blakemore Evans, and Arthur Freeman deal with dissimilar topics, but all three write with a sense of editorial original sin — of the inevitability of past error and (for Evans and Freeman) of future stumbles — and of the amount of basic editorial work still to be done. Proudfoot, for example, considering the dramatic manuscripts remaining to us from the English Renaissance, points out that a number have yet to appear in reliable modern editions. Moreover, the lessons these manuscripts have for us, in our editing of Renaissance printed texts, have not by any means all been learned. Proudfoot suggests that identification of manuscript characteristics which might commonly have resulted in errors in Renaissance printed texts – for example, the similarity in Elizabethan secretary hand between *e* and *d*, especially in final position – together with qualitative and quantitative analysis of the errors contained in printed texts could be of considerable importance in an editor's consideration of particular emendations to his printed copy-text. He also criticizes mid-twentieth-century "excessive concentration [in textual studies] on matters of sometimes fruitless speculation and on bibliographical techniques . . . of limited practical utility."

G. Blakemore Evans, because focusing on Shakespeare and on the enormous volume of textual work done on Shakespeare's plays from the seventeenth century on, reacts above all in his paper to what he calls "the burden of the past:" the work of former textual critics, good and bad, which the modern editor of Shakespeare must take into account. The past work hinders the modern editor in his attempt to approach the texts with a fresh, unprejudiced look at the original readings and at possible corrections, though it also of course provides good and bad examples of emendations to follow or to shun, considered principles to study, and more than the occasional inspiration. Evans both begins and ends pessimistically, with the suggestion that the modern editor cannot in fact restore Shakespeare's text to its original form; despite our best efforts, the original is irretrievably lost.

The papers of both Proudfoot and Evans, and of the other speakers as well, are excellent examples of the concern with minor details of text which must be the hallmark of a good editor. Evans and Corrigan, for example, comment at length on problems of punctuation. The difficult decisions involved in punctuation interpretation and modernization can often consume a very large amount of the editor's time and attention (in modernized texts); and it must be a rare editor indeed who has never found himself changing several punctuation marks back and forth, through several sets of textual checks and even proofs, unable to make the final irrevocable decision between comma and semicolon, semicolon and period, until forced by time or the publisher into dissatisfied quiescence. Punctuation—spelling—capitalization: over such matters do ardent editors not only of opposing schools (fidelity to copy-text; selective modernization; total modernization) but even of the same school come to blows.

Beatrice Corrigan, in her paper on Italian Renaissance dramatic texts, turns our attention to the research opportunities for future editing work in the field. Major plays have in the past been poorly edited, austerely edited, or not edited at all; properly annotated texts have been at a minimum; and problems in the matter of choice of copy-text, above all because of unscrupulous early printers, also should lure into the field any scholar interested in editing. The problems of modernization (and Corrigan agrees with the practice of "discreet modernization")—in capitalization, spelling, punctuation, and so forth—also loom large. And finally, who could resist the challenge of attempting to be an annotator such as Corrigan demands: one, for example, of the comedies, with intimate knowledge of the authors' cities—their laws, customs, dialects, and contemporary history?

Whereas Corrigan looks above all to the future, Arnold G. Reichenberger presents largely a detailed account of past achievements in the editing of Spanish seventeenth-century *comedias*. The multiplicity of seventeenth-century editions, together with the enormous output of dramatists such as Lope de Vega, creates the first and most staggering editorial problem in the field: the sheer volume of the material to be examined and mastered. Problems of punctuation pale into insignificance when a single seventeenth-century volume of plays may exist in fifteen early editions within twenty-three years, and when an author such as Lope de Vega may have over three hundred *comedias* still extant. Early collections of plays also exist which were published over a period of, for example, some forty-three years. Unscrupulous early booksellers have compounded the problems. Not surprisingly, as a result "no critical edition of the total work of any playwright has [yet] been attempted."

At the Conference itself Arthur Freeman's paper began the Saturday session on a note of scepticism and of provocation. In this volume Freeman's paper comes fittingly at the close, as both a caveat and a challenge for the future. Error has been with us, in printed texts of plays, from the original Renaissance editions through the most careful of modern editions; it creeps in at any and every stage of the transmission process. We can reduce modern types of error through better knowledge of modern methods of transmission (for example, of typing, and of reproduction from photographs) and the kinds of mistakes to which they typically lead. We can encourage critics and reviewers to hunt for errors in the published work, for later correction. But perhaps the time has come for editors to cease anguishing over inevitable mistakes and misinterpretations and simply to get on with the job of providing the best texts possible, errors and all, without delay and with what Freeman terms "the wise commentary, the just evaluation, and the illuminating critical perspective" that is probably the major part, in any case, of a full, modern, critical edition of a Renaissance dramatic text. Without such commentary, though with the best methods of emendation, modernization, punctuation, and capitalization, does not any modern edition of a Renaissance play run the risk of being "the name, and not the thing"?[1]—the mere reproduction, and not the necessary recreation, of the living drama the editor himself has come to know and, in his enthusiastic knowledge and appreciation, is attempting to pass on to others? The final lesson may be that although error cannot be avoided it can—and should—be surmounted.

The Committee of the Conference on Editorial Problems extends its thanks to both The Canada Council and the University of Toronto for the generous financial help which made this year's Conference possible. As convenor of the 1975 Conference I also owe personal thanks, for their help, to the other members of the Conference Committee: G.E. Bentley, Jr., Alan Dainard, Hugo de Quehen, Eric Domville, David Esplin, Francess Halpenny, Robin Jackson, John McClelland, George Rigg, John Robson, and especially Michael Sidnell. And thanks of course go above all to our five speakers, for sharing their convictions and doubts with us, and for thus provoking much immediate discussion and long-term thought on the editorial problems that alternately plague and delight us all.

[1] *All's Well That Ends Well*, V.iii. 307-8: *The Riverside Shakespeare*, eds. G.B. Evans, H. Levin, H. Baker, A. Barton, F. Kermode, H. Smith, M. Edel (Boston, 1974).

DRAMATIC MANUSCRIPTS
AND THE EDITOR

G.R. Proudfoot

Alvin Kernan, introducing his section of Volume III of
the new *Revels History of Drama in English,* which covers
the period 1576-1613, takes comfort from the thought
that "A writer of a history of this period begins . . . with
excellent bibliography and superb texts." The range of
editions cited in his text bears out his claim, especially if
their profusion be counted among the excellences of
recent editions of Elizabethan plays, but his quotations
may raise a question in the mind of the general reader.
Why are the works of Shakespeare and Marlowe quoted in
modern spelling and those of other playwrights, Jonson
among them, in original spelling? The answer which might
be offered is that the editors of Elizabethan plays, of
whom more must be alive at this moment than at any
previous time, perceive a divided duty and are to be
recognized by their emblem of one auspicious and one
dropping eye—or, to improve my credentials—*an* auspicious and *a* dropping eye. With the auspicious eye they
look to the immediate needs of their public, the students
of English literature and the acting companies of the
English-speaking world, to whom it is their duty to offer
the best and most intelligible texts of their authors. With
the other eye, dropping from long hours of collation and
flickering with a perceptible Hinmanic tick, they regard
the glacierlike advancement of textual and bibliographical

knowledge, to which their own labours with a particular
text or author may be hoped to add an icicle. After considering some more general aspects of my topic, I shall try
to suggest a way—somewhat neglected of late—in which
editors may both help themselves towards a fuller understanding of their texts and contribute to the solution of
some broader problems of the editing of Elizabethan
plays.

In Elizabethan studies, "dramatic manuscripts" is a term
which covers a wide range of documents, including
manuscript play texts of many and various kinds, dates
and origins, as well as the small and miscellaneous selection of other manuscripts relating to plays and to their
performance which have survived, against all the odds,
from the late sixteenth and early seventeenth centuries—
players' parts, for example, and "plots," both those used
to control performances and one or two scraps of
"author's plots" or scenarios for plays to be written.
Among the play texts are complete plays written for the
companies of professional players (some in the hands of
their authors, some scribal copies) many of which reveal,
from the manner in which they have been annotated, that
they were either used as prompt-books or at least marked
up to provide the basic texts from which prompt-books
could then be copied. Their importance derives, in some
cases, from their status as witnesses (often the sole witnesses) for texts of real literary and dramatic merit, but
more generally from their unique character as sources of
information about the composition of plays and their
transmission in manuscript and for the amount of detail
that can be gleaned from the "prompt" manuscripts about
particular dramatic companies and their personnel, both
actors and scribes. Their importance for editors lies not
only in these general considerations but in the fact that
whereas every printed play that is was manuscript once,

the vast majority of extant plays survive only in print, leaving unanswered (and perhaps unanswerable) many vexing questions about the lost manuscripts which served as printer's copy for them. It follows that the study of dramatic manuscripts is an essential part of the training of any editor of Elizabethan drama and that we may do well to take an occasional look back at what we have been doing with these documents which axiomatically "form an indispensable background to all useful thought, and a framework to which must conform all valid conjecture, concerning the textual phenomena and history of the Elizabethan drama."[1]

My quotation, of course, points at once to a predicament inherent in my choice of topic. The words are those of Sir Walter Greg, the scholar who did more than any before him to illuminate and make available for scholarly purposes the surviving documents of the Elizabethan theatre and who left for those who follow, not indeed nothing to do, but at least a task whose continuation into the resources remaining must look like the addition of appendices to the corpus of his work. Greg's words come from one of his most substantial contributions to the subject, his *Dramatic Documents from the Elizabethan Playhouses,* which he published in 1931, midway in a career well begun in the 1890s and actively continued until his death early in 1959. When he wrote the words, Greg had already published editions of several play texts from manuscript. These included that most celebrated of all Elizabethan play manuscripts, *The Book of Sir Thomas More,* which he edited for the Malone Society in 1911, having first tried his hand on *The Second Maiden's Tragedy* (a play which some would attribute to Thomas Middleton) in 1909. During his years as its founding

---

[1]W.W. Greg, *Dramatic Documents from the Elizabethan Playhouses* (Oxford, 1931), p.xi.

General Editor (1906-1939), the Malone Society published editions of fourteen major Elizabethan play manuscripts and a number of others of earlier date or of amateur provenance, all of them "checked by the General Editor." Apart from his editions, Greg's main contributions to the subject included his leading role in the compilation, transcription and annotation of the volumes of *English Literary Autographs, 1550-1650;*[2] his comparison of the player's part of "Orlando" from Robert Greene's *Orlando Furioso* and the "plot" of George Peele's *The Battle of Alcazar* with the printed texts of the two plays;[3] his description and classification of the manuscripts relating to the professional companies in *Dramatic Documents*; and last, but not least, his numerous contributions, in books, articles and reviews, to the question of the lost manuscripts underlying the texts of printed plays. His last extended survey of the subject, in chapters 3 and 4 of *The Shakespeare First Folio* (Oxford, 1955), was the product of a sixty-year involvement with it and remains, twenty years later, an inevitable point of departure for any attempt to extend the discussion of dramatic manuscripts.

In emphasizing Greg's contribution to the study of these manuscripts, I would not wish to distract attention from the very substantial contributions made to the subject by others. These others include the succession of editors of manuscript plays for the Malone Society both under Greg's General Editorship and under that of his successors, F.P. Wilson and Arthur Brown, themselves respectively editors of such major manuscripts as Ralph Crane's transcripts of Thomas Middleton's *The Witch* and John Fletcher's *Demetrius and Enanthe,* and the difficult autograph manu-

[2]Oxford, 1932 [1925-32].

[3]*Two Elizabethan Stage Abridgements: The Battle of Alcazar & Orlando Furioso* (Oxford, 1922).

script of Thomas Heywood's comedy *The Captives*.[4]
Among these editors were two scholars who were to make
their own distinctive contributions to the study of Shakespeare's texts and the lost manuscripts underlying them.
One was John Dover Wilson, whose analysis of *The Manuscript of Shakespeare's "Hamlet" and the Problems of its
Transmission* (Cambridge, 1934) was a landmark in Shakespearian textual studies, and whose "Notes on the Text"
in his *New Cambridge Shakespeare* retain the excitement
of their author's energy and enthusiasm though sometimes
apprehending rather more than cool reason can compre-
hend. The other, C.J. Sisson, prepared the Malone
Society's edition (Oxford, 1927) of Philip Massinger's
autograph manuscript of *Believe As You List*, with the
prompt-annotations of the scribe then referred to as
"Jhon" (later identified by J. Gerritsen as Edward Knight,
book-keeper of the King's Men in the 1620s[5]). Sisson's
edition of Shakespeare and its sizeable parergon, the two
volumes of *New Readings in Shakespeare* (Cambridge,
1956), reflected a concern for manuscripts which was felt
by many to have been carried too far for conviction. That
his attempts to solve Shakespearian cruces by palaeo-
graphic demonstration should have provoked more scepticism than applause was perhaps to be expected of a
generation whose reaction against the whimsical eclecticism of earlier editorial tradition has tended to elevate a
modest and self-effacing conversatism (often appropriate
to textual situations where all that we can define is the
extent of our ignorance) into a principle of self-defensive
aggression. The record of Sisson's successes is to be read in
the textual apparatus of the editions of Shakespeare
published since 1956.

[4]Malone Society Reprints (Oxford, 1948 (1950); 1950 (1951); 1953).

[5]J. Gerritsen, ed., *The Honest Man's Fortune* (Groningen, Djakarta, 1952).

Of the others who devoted their attention to Elizabethan dramatic manuscripts, none made a more significant contribution than R.C. Bald, whose work on the Lambarde manuscripts of Thomas Middleton's *Hengist, King of Kent,* two "Beaumont and Fletcher" plays, *The Beggars' Bush* and *The Woman's Prize,* Sir William Berkeley's *The Lost Lady* and Arthur Wilson's *The Inconstant Lady,*[6] began to supplement Greg's survey by describing the main items in the most important of the manuscript collections which Greg did not see. The Lambarde collection, untraceable when Greg was writing his *Dramatic Documents* since its sale in 1924, was acquired by Henry Clay Folger and is now in the Folger Library. Bald's edition of *Hengist* (New York and London, 1938) complemented that of Middleton's *A Game at Chess,* from the autograph manuscript at Trinity College, Cambridge, which he had published in 1929.

That the briefest survey of dramatic manuscripts should have so much to say of the editing of them in the present century is hardly remarkable, as many had never been printed before and of those that had, few had been so edited as to afford reliable reading texts, let alone texts scrupulous enough in detail to provide a basis for detailed investigation of any kind. Not the least of Greg's contributions to the study of dramatic manuscripts was his establishment, by example, of adequate standards of care and accuracy in their editing. Nor is the task of editing by any means finished: manuscript plays described by Greg in 1931 but as yet unavailable in reliable scholarly editions include *The Wasp,* from Alnwick Castle; *The Faithful Friends,* from the Dyce collection in the Victoria and

---

[6]*Bibliographical Studies in the Beaumont and Fletcher Folio* (London, 1938); "Sir William Berkeley's *The Lost Lady,*" *The Library,* 4th series, XVII (1937), 395-426; "Arthur Wilson's *The Inconstant Lady,*" *ibid.,* XVIII (1938), 287-313.

Albert Museum; Thomas Heywood's autograph transcript of *The Escapes of Jupiter* from the largest of all early seventeenth-century manuscript collections of plays, MS. Egerton 1994 in the British Library; the Lambarde manuscripts, except for *Hengist;* and the six plays of that eccentric and tireless amateur playwright, William Percy, in the last and most complete of three extant autograph collections, now in the Huntington Library. This list neither exhausts the plays described by Greg nor takes account of others which have come to light more recently, of which the most interesting are probably the anonymous Caroline comedy, *Wit's Triumvirate, or the Philosopher,* presented to the British Museum in 1942, and the play of *Tom a Lincoln* (perhaps to be attributed to Thomas Heywood) which was found at Melbourne Hall, Derbyshire, in 1973. Nor have I made much mention of the numerous manuscript plays unconnected with the professional companies: school and college plays, in English, Latin or even Greek; amateur plays; and dramatic entertainments of all kinds. The researches of Alfred Harbage, consolidated by those of Samuel Schoenbaum in his revisions of Harbage's *Annals of English Drama, 975-1700,*[7] have made more readily available than before the names and whereabouts of a surprisingly large number of documents dating from before 1700 and broadly describable as "dramatic manuscripts." That all, or even most, of the less-known items in their census are of a literary merit to recommend their publication is unlikely, but the likelihood is far greater that among them lie the answers to some unanswered questions about scribes, authorship, lost printer's-copy manuscripts or theatrical history, which may even bear on our study of the major drama of the time. Editions

[7]London, 1964; with Supplements (Evanston, Illinois, 1966 and 1970).

of many of them are in preparation, some of them for the Malone Society.

Even so summary an account must confirm the view that the importance of manuscript play texts and their study is fundamental. Not only are we now able to read some three dozen plays in editions which give a reliable sense of the manuscripts from which they are printed, but we can turn to facsimiles, and in some cases to detailed palaeographical analyses, of the hands of a number of important playwrights, Thomas Middleton, Philip Massinger, Thomas Heywood, Anthony Munday, Thomas Dekker and Henry Chettle among them, as well as to those of at least four scribes employed either on an occasional or regular basis by dramatic companies from the 1590s to the 1620s, among them Ralph Crane, whose work for the King's Men included the transcription of five texts to provide printer's copy for the first Folio of Shakespeare, and Edward Knight, who was for some years the King's Men's book-keeper. The methods and aims of the censorship of plays under successive Masters of the Revels, from Edmund Tilney to Henry Herbert, are more graphically represented in some of these manuscripts than they could be elsewhere, and the notes of actors' names found in those annotated as prompt-books have made a large contribution to the history of the companies involved.

In relation to the editing of plays, the manuscripts have offered evidence of the existence of a number of different kinds of text, any one of which, we may suppose, could in the right circumstances have become copy for a printed edition. The classification of these types and the description of the characteristic features of each has been a continuing preoccupation of textual scholars, and the terms "foul papers," "fair copy," "prompt-book," "presentation copy" and "memorial transcript" have made the schools ring since it has become possible to support their use by reference to particular examples of each type. Indeed, the attempt to identify the class to which the lost copy-manuscript underlying a printed edition belonged has become one of the major endeavours of textual scholarship and no edition with pretensions to scholarly adequacy is now published without some hypothetical statement on this score.

The questions which face editors of Elizabethan plays today are the same questions that faced their predecessors, but the last fifty years have seen both unprecedented activity and unprecedented ingenuity in the devising of techniques for getting the texts themselves, often our major, if not sole, source of information, to yield up their secrets. These techniques have necessarily been applied to the early witnesses themselves, manuscript and printed, and have concentrated on their physical composition and on the methods of production which brought them into being, with consequential effects on the texts which they transmit. Bibliographical analysis has yielded results of such consistent, and occasionally spectacular, significance that it came, for a while, to seem to be a skeleton key to all textual mysteries. The study of the manuscripts has pursued a parallel, if less often contentious, course, until we have reached a point at which we have a sufficient sense of the early history of the transmission of play-texts to approach the old task of editing them with, at least, a new awareness of the difficulties inherent in the exercise and of the quality of our own ignorance in approaching it.

To gauge the kind of progress achieved, it may suffice to select a few of the more speculative papers published during the past half-century and to see how their suggestions have been borne out or rendered obsolete by the progress of research. In picking three such papers for brief comment, I have my own topic very much in mind: they are C.J. Sisson's "Bibliographical Aspects of Some

Stuart Dramatic Manuscripts," published in the first
volume of *The Review of English Studies* (1925); R.B.
McKerrow's "A Suggestion Regarding Shakespeare's
Manuscripts," in *Review of English Studies*, XI (1935);
and "New Approaches to Textual Problems in Shakespeare," contributed by Philip Williams to the eighth
volume (1956) of *Studies in Bibliography*. Each writer was
concerned with the relation between plays surviving only
in print and the lost manuscripts lying behind them.

In 1925, Sisson, remarking on the exciting approaches
to this problem, from the direction of the printed text,
which Dover Wilson was initiating in the early volumes
of his *New Shakespeare,* offered in turn, and as something
of a novelty, the suggestion that the study of manuscripts,
which existed in "a surprising number and variety,"
might help the bibliographers "to arrive at a classified
analysis of the types of bibliographical anomalies likely
to occur" in print, which might "be a valuable guide to
conjecture and serve either to check or to confirm the
results of the direct method of approach." He noted that
"the one thing missing is an actual printer's copy. No
manuscript has survived the handling of the compositor."
He also mentioned, as "a great desideratum," "A descriptive hand-list of all the extant plays." To take the last
points first: while no copy manuscript of a play has yet
appeared, the small number of other printer's-copy manuscripts is gradually increasing (although the study of them
is still oddly neglected). Greg's *Dramatic Documents* went
some way towards providing the check-list.

Sisson chose for further comment three of the manuscripts in the Dyce collection, Massinger's autograph
Believe As You List and "two manuscript copies of plays
by Fletcher," *The Honest Man's Fortune* and *The Faithful
Friends*. His aim was to reveal in these manuscripts irregularities analogous to, and therefore potentially sources

of, those found in printed plays. His four classes of irregularity were: "false verse-lining," which he found in
passages by both Massinger and "the stage-adaptor" in
Believe As You List; "repeated passages," which he found
indicating the beginning and end of a cut in *The Faithful
Friends*; "ghost parts," whose possible origin he tried to
identify in the "stage-adaptor's" reduction of Massinger's
named minor roles to fit his casting; and "variant speech-
headings," which were limited, in these manuscripts, to
variations between Massinger and the "adaptor" in the
spelling of some characters' names. It is in the generality of
its terms that this article most immediately reveals its
date, but it does so also by the assumption of a simple
one-to-one relationship between manuscripts and what a
compositor was likely to set in type: we have learned
more since—not wholly to our comfort. Both bibliographical research and work on the manuscripts have changed
the detail of the picture too: faulty verse-lining in printed
texts now at once suggests erroneous "casting-off" of copy
rather than fidelity to erroneous copy; equally, the "stage-
adaptor" is now more clearly visible as Edward Knight,
book-keeper of the King's Men, marking up his author's
"fair copy" as a prompt-book.

McKerrow's "Suggestion Regarding Shakespeare's Manuscripts" was an unobtrusive bomb-shell, containing in its
six pages the outlines of positions still central to the
orthodox view of Shakespearian textual matters (however
far they may have needed—and may still need—to be
qualified and extended). His simple perception—simple,
at least, in retrospect—was that major irregularities in the
naming and description of characters in a printed play
text, especially in its speech prefixes, which had previously
been considered as evidence of progressive corruption,
could be most plausibly accounted for as a feature of the
author's own manuscript, written in course of composi-

tion, whereas corresponding regularity might be the fingerprint of a scribe, especially if the copy he was making were designed to serve as a prompt-book. The general implication for editors of the two classes of printed text thus distinguished, of which he offered six Shakespearian examples in each class, was that

In the one case we must allow for confused corrections and careless writing, but can take it for granted that the compositor had before him something which, though perhaps difficult to decipher, embodied the intention of the author, and that the text as we have it must represent fairly closely what the manuscript *looked like* to the compositor. In the other case the compositor would presumably be working from a manuscript which would in itself be easily legible, but the text of which might already have been tampered with by someone who had views as to what the author ought to have written, and who placed the construction of a readable text above the duty of following closely the *ductus litterarum* of his original. The kinds of error which we should expect to find in prints from manuscripts of the two groups may evidently be very different.[8]

It might be claimed, without undue exaggeration, that the subsequent course of forty years (so far) of Shakespearian textual research was adumbrated in those two sentences. McKerrow wrote them after Greg had published his *Dramatic Documents*, with its first full-scale attempt to classify the surviving manuscripts, and his avoidance of any more precise distinction between authorial and scribal manuscripts must have resulted from a deliberate decision. Later, in his *Prolegomena for the Oxford Shakespeare*,[9] he was to express grave doubts of the utility of speculation about the character of the lost manuscripts. Paradoxically, Greg's own constant awareness of the problems of classi-

[8]*Review of English Studies*, XI (1935), 465.
[9]Oxford, 1939, pp. 9-10.

fication posed by even the surviving manuscripts, let alone the lost ones, did not prevent him from attempting a survey of the likely character of the lost manuscripts underlying the substantive early editions of Shakespeare, and his own extremely tentative suggestions became the point of departure for continuing efforts, notably on the part of Fredson Bowers,[10] to refine on Greg's classifications and to posit a degree of certainty in this most speculative of areas which, if not merely unattainable, is at least, in all but a very few instances, far beyond our reach in the present state of our knowledge. Of the few exceptions, the five First Folio comedies believed to have been set from transcripts in the hand of Ralph Crane have received the most attention, mainly because enough manuscripts in his hand have survived to afford a substantial basis for this investigation, but also because the study of the compositors who set the First Folio is sufficiently advanced for the fine discrimination of their preferred verbal forms from Crane's to be feasible. The findings of the latest investigator of Crane, T.H. Howard-Hill, strikingly echo and vindicate McKerrow's characterization of the effects a scribe might be expected to have on a play text.[11]

The investigation of Ralph Crane was made possible by the gradual discovery of seven dramatic manuscripts in his hand, dating from 1618 to 1625. No comparable body of material exists in the hand of any other writer likely to have written manuscripts from which plays were printed, although two other scribes are represented by two manuscript plays each, Edward Knight by *The Honest Man's Fortune* and a transcript of the "foul papers" of Fletcher's

---

[10]*On Editing Shakespeare and the Elizabethan Dramatists* (London, 1955), pp. 10-12.

[11]*Ralph Crane and Some Shakespeare First Folio Comedies* (Charlottesville, 1972), pp. 138-40.

Bonduca (as well as by his minor contributions in *Believe As You List* and elsewhere), and a scribe employed by the Cockpit company in the 1630s by *The Welsh Ambassador,* attributed to Thomas Dekker, and Massinger's *The Parliament of Love.* The identifiable characteristics of Knight, and of those authors whose autographs we have, have so far been used only sporadically, mainly by editors of single plays in which those writers may have been involved. In view of the small number of manuscripts involved, it is surprising that no more systematic analysis of identified authorial hands and habits has yet been attempted as a preliminary to the search for those printed texts in which their stigmata may be identified. The great exception, here as elsewhere, is Shakespeare, although, as recent articles have revealed, even *The Book of Sir Thomas More* and "Hand D's" contribution to it are not closed subjects for research.[12]

Of course a main deterrent, apart from the lack of easily available and reliable editions of all the relevant manuscripts—no edition exists, for instance, of Middleton's autograph portion of the Bridgewater manuscript of his *A Game at Chess* (Huntington Library)—has been an awareness of the prior need for dependable analyses of the compositors in all the printed plays in question. Philip Williams, writing in the mid-1950s, had at his disposal the compositor analyses of the Shakespeare First Folio available at that date, notably those of Alice Walker.[13] He saw that the identification of compositors would make it possible to begin to isolate those "characteristics of the

[12]P.W.M. Blayney, "*The Booke of Sir Thomas Moore* Re-Examined," *Studies in Philology*, LXIX (1972), 167-91; M.L. Hays, "Watermarks in the Manuscript of *Sir Thomas More*," *Shakespeare Quarterly*, XXVI (1975), 66-9.

[13]See *Textual Problems of the First Folio* (Cambridge, 1953).

manuscript" which "were preserved, perhaps quite inadvertently" in the twenty-four Folio plays held by Greg to have been set from manuscript copy. He noticed, for instance, that "contradictions and inconsistencies" in the text of *Henry VI*, Part I, particularly in its stage directions, which had seemed to Greg to suggest "Either composite authorship or revision," could be explained by the division of type-setting between Compositor A, who set most of Acts I to III and was faithful to copy, and Compositor B (his role as villain beginning to take shape) who set most of Acts IV and V and "revamped" the stage directions—which he "was, as we know from his work elsewhere, quite capable of doing." Williams likewise suggested that a study of those twenty-four plays "as a group as well as individually" was a necessary step towards discriminating between spellings to be attributed to the preferences of individual compositors and others which might then emerge as copy-spellings. He instanced the odd behaviour of compositors A and B in setting the exclamation "oh": in *Julius Caesar*, both set "o"; in *The Comedy of Errors,* both set "oh"; whereas in *Troilus and Cressida,* both alternated between the two spellings. His conclusion was that in each case both compositors were following copy-spellings. In fact, his example merely underlines the need for reliable compositor identifications as a first step towards closer analysis of the spellings in a printed text. We are now told that the Compositor A to whom Alice Walker and Hinman assigned a large share in the Folio comedies was not the same man as the A of the Folio histories and tragedies.[14] Those pages have been reassigned to C, D and, most recently, a hitherto-unknown sixth man, F. A's stint in *The Comedy of Errors* is now divided

[14]See T.H. Howard-Hill, "The Compositors of Shakespeare's Folio Comedies," *Studies in Bibliography*, XXVI (1973), 61-106.

between C and D, which may leave Williams' essential point intact, but destroys the argument by which he reached it.

Williams realized the importance of compositor analysis for another kind of investigation depending on linguistic minutiae, that of the authorship of anonymous or collaborative plays, pointing out that investigators of *Henry VIII* who regarded alternations between "them" and "'em" or "you" and "ye" as discriminators between the hands of Shakespeare and Fletcher would have to take careful account of the relatively greater frequency of "Fletcher" forms in the pages set by the conservative A as against B's pages, from which the compositor might be deemed to have removed some of the evidence. Above all, he was aware that a compositor's errors and his departures from strongly established preferences should be regarded as affording potential evidence about his lost copy manuscript. He concluded:

When the varnish of the folio compositors has been removed, the grain of the underlying manuscripts will be revealed in its true color. Then, and not until then, shall we have exhausted the evidence possible about the kinds of copy from which these plays were set. I may be too optimistic, but I venture to hope that when the job is done, we shall be able to distinguish those plays which were set from Shakespeare's holograph from those set from scribal transcripts, and to assign with some certainty the transcripts to the scribes that made them. A good place to start will be with the five plays which are now thought to have been set from transcripts made by Ralph Crane. [15]

Williams may indeed have been too optimistic; certainly Alice Walker was when, in the previous year, she expressed the hope that within two or three years compositor iden-

[15] *Studies in Bibliography*, VIII (1956), 11-12.

tifications for the whole corpus of Elizabethan printed drama might be established and the full and comprehensive analysis of the spellings in dramatic texts begun.[16] But the achievements of the past twenty years have been considerable, especially with Shakespeare: the work of Charlton Hinman on the printing and proof-reading of the First Folio and that of others in refining on his analysis of the compositors; the publication of the first really reliable facsimile of the Folio; the analysis of the printing of many of the good quartos and the study of the printing-houses which produced them; the computer-concording of the substantive editions of Shakespeare in their original spelling and the making of the electronic tapes on which the concordances are based; these and many other bibliographical researches bearing less directly on the drama have gradually increased our understanding and control of the detail of Shakespeare's text. But with the increased understanding comes also an increasing sense that the removal of the varnish may (to modify the metaphor) involve the loss of some paint too and that we may, in the end, face large patches of bare canvas.

While the progress of bibliographical and linguistic analysis of plays holds the promise of final answers to some large questions about the transmission of texts, authorship and chronology, individual editors of texts may still find more direct ways in which the extant manuscripts may serve their purposes. To hazard a generalization: whereas knowledge, at once as wide and as precise as can be achieved, about all the transmitting agents, whether authors or scribes, compositors or proof-readers, will be necessary if the large questions are to be answered, the practical and immediate needs of the editor, faced, as

[16]"Compositor Determination and other Problems in Shakespearian Texts," *Studies in Bibliography*, VII (1955), 3-15.

always, with small and particular questions, may often be supplied by cheaper means. For many, maybe even most, normal editorial purposes, it is more important to know of the usual types of error to which scribes and compositors were prone than to reach any degree of confidence about the identity of the particular transmitting agents of a given text or passage. Equally, even where uncertainty persists about the precise identity of the compositors of a printed play or about the nature of the lost copy manuscript, some characteristics of that lost copy manuscript may be identifiable.

A brief look at some details from two manuscript plays and a handful of printed ones will amplify and may clarify my point.

The first manuscript contains a Caroline comedy of unknown authorship, *The Wasp, or Subjects' Precedent*, in the collection of the Duke of Northumberland at Alnwick Castle, of which the first printed edition, prepared by J.W. Lever, is shortly to be published by the Malone Society. As Professor Lever has already published a general account of the play,[17] I may perhaps limit my reference to selected features of it. That the principal hand in the manuscript is that of the author is not in doubt, nor that the play has been marked up for production and cut—in places quite heavily—by a second hand, evidently that of a theatrical book-keeper, in all probability the same man who added prompt annotation to Henry Glapthorne's *The Lady Mother*[18] which, like *The Wasp*, was written for the King's Revels Company in the mid-1630s. Whether the manuscript should properly be classified as "foul papers" (for which much of it seems too tidy), or "fair copy" (which

[17]"*The Wasp*: A Trial Flight," in *The Elizabethan Theatre IV*, ed. G.R. Hibbard (Waterloo, Ontario, 1974).

[18]Ed. A. Brown, Malone Society Reprints (Oxford, 1958 (1959)).

passages of heavy deletion and re-writing must forbid), or "prompt-copy" (for which it appears too disordered), or merely "author's papers with prompt-annotation," is a nice question—which may safely be allowed to remain open. Whether the play was licensed and, if so, whether any of the many marks of deletion and marginal crosses to be found in it reflect the opinions of a licenser, remains uncertain, as the final leaf, which might have borne the licence of Henry Herbert or his deputy, is missing; some few verbal alterations in a third hand could conceivably be the work of a licenser. Had it been printed in the 1630s, *The Wasp* might have shown all the symptoms of "prompt-book" copy: advance warnings for entrances, or double music cues, for example, together with some details which an alert editor might have spotted as the symptoms of authorial copy. A faithful compositor would have been taxed by several passages of heavy deletion and interlined revision, especially where these involved dislocation of the verse-lining. He would also have had to work out for himself the correct position of two verse lines added vertically in the outer margin of folio 16 verso. In several other marginal additions, he might have found dialogue and stage directions hard to distinguish. Had he paid any attention to copy in such matters, he would have found the punctuation generally adequate but might have wondered what the writer's intentions were in the matter of capitalization, as the writer fluctuates between distinct majuscule forms and minuscule forms of varying size, and variously flourished, without any appearance of system. Although his eye would have been more familiar with the predominantly English hand of the author than is that of a modern editor, he might have experienced some at least of the difficulties which led to disagreement and sometimes bafflement during the preparation of the Malone Society text. Certain letter-forms or combinations might easily have induced error, particularly in the early stages of type-setting, before the hand became familiar: these include the use of a majuscule *M* with the form of *N*; the sporadic use of a long-*s* form for minuscule *h* before certain other letters; a normal formation of minuscule *o* nearly identical with *e*, and an *oo* form sometimes barely distinguishable from *a*. Minim errors, especially the writing of too many or too few minim strokes in words with combinations of successive *i, m, n,* and *u,* are frequent in the authorial hand. The formation of *r* as *c* on two occasions is either simply erroneous or evidence of another anomalous habit. Initial *no-* or *ni-* is sometimes so like *w-* as to admit of easy confusion. Usually the context dictates the correct reading so far as substance, rather than merely spelling, is con-cerned, but where unusual words or proper names are involved, dependence on the letter-forms would have been a compositor's only resource. My own intervention as compositor might easily have led to the vulgarization to "whoremonger," misspelt "whemonger," of the word which Lever rightly deciphered as the unusual "Nozemon-ger" ("noose-monger"), a jocular synonym for a hangman (1.764). In editing such a text the peculiarities of the hand, or hands, should be described as precisely as possible, even if many of them, such as minim errors, may seem commonplace, as they draw attention to potential sources of error in printed texts of the same date and may, in combination, be found distinctive enough to become identifying marks for the lost copy of printed plays. The *N*-formed majuscule *M* is, I suspect, among the rarer fea-tures of this hand, but can be matched in at least one printed play. That it may also have occurred in the hand of the writer of the additions to *Mucedorus* first printed in William Jones's quarto of 1610 is suggested by the capitali-zation and spelling of "Neager" for "meager" in the final addition (F3), though, less plausibly, the error could be traced to a misreading of minuscule minims. The page on which it is found also contains the misreading "Comict" for "Comick," in what is otherwise a careful and correct piece of type-setting, suggesting the limitations of the compositor's vocabulary.

The Dyce manuscript of *The Faithful Friends*, a play still lingering uneasily on the fringes of the Beaumont and Fletcher canon, and of quite uncertain date, authorship and provenance, is a scribal transcript, lacking leaves at the beginning and end which must have been removed by an early owner, in the eighteenth century, at which time they were replaced by leaves bearing a copy of the opening and closing lines in a hand of that period. It lacks prompt-annotation, but the main body of the text has been sporadically altered, amplified and cut in an informal and untidy hand, which may be authorial. Not all the corrections in the manuscript are attributable to this second hand, many being clearly identifiable as the work of the eighteenth-century hand which supplied the transcripts of the missing leaves. This late corrector has "improved" the scribe's spelling, put right most of his errors with classical names and supplemented his punctuation, most assiduously in a scene of bawdry which bristles with his disapproving commas and lascivious semi-colons. Other stray corrections and deletions and the underlining of several passages in a reddish ink, perhaps to indicate deletion, can hardly be attributed to particular writers, nor is their date or intention always apparent. The most discussed scene in the play, numbered by earlier editors Act IV, scene v, is absent from the transcript, where its contents are summarized under the heading of "The Plott of a Scene of mirth to conclude this fourth Acte." Dialogue for the scene is supplied on a single quarto leaf interleaved at this point in the manuscript and written in a hand not found elsewhere in it, which may be that of an author in course of composition. If this hand is authorial, and the leaf of dialogue original, then we have possible evidence for collaborative authorship of *The Faithful Friends*. That the play, or at least this manuscript of it, was abandoned before production seems to be the inevitable inference to be drawn from progressive marks of cutting which end up by reducing to nothing a crucial scene (III.ii), in which the malcontent soldier Rufinus woos the virtuous Philadelpha in the suit of the King (whose virtuous intention of testing them both is not revealed until the final act). Whether the cuts were made in response to objections from the Master of the Revels or in anticipation of such objections can hardly be determined in the absence of the original final leaf.

Here again we have a manuscript of mixed type: a scribal transcript bearing no unambiguous marks of theatrical use and including one leaf of what may be "foul papers." Scribal features which might have shown through in print are the imprecise lining of many speech prefixes, which could have led an inattentive compositor to misattribute speeches or lines; the lacunae in the text where the scribe found his exemplar illegible (some of which were filled by the various correcting hands); and the reduction to nonsense of what we may assume to have been accurate classical allusions in that exemplar, such as "by men" for "Hymen" (1.685) and "Hyther boreans" for "Hyperboreans" (1.2281). The scribe's hand, unlike that of the principal corrector, is a fairly neat and legible Italian one, though it poses the usual problem about capitalization and uses the potentially confusing "nn" form for "un." Illegible words occasionally result from the correction of the scribe's first attempt either by himself or by the main corrector. That this corrector may be an author is suggested not only by the general nature of his alterations, but also by a detail of spelling. At one point (1.2542), he has added a phrase involving the word "entranced," which he spells "jntrancet;" this same spelling of "-et" for "-ed" is also found four times in the scribal transcript, strongly suggesting that it is an authorial form retained by the scribe ("pacet" 1.91; "disgracet" 1.1246; "forcet" 1.2429; and "placet" 1.2500). An interesting implication of this detail is that it affords presumable evidence of an eccentric authorial spelling surviving in a scribal transcript.

In spite of some obvious overlap, the types of difficulty that these two manuscripts would have presented to a seventeenth-century compositor (and do present to a twentieth-century editor) suggest, not so much general principles which would serve the editor of printed plays, as possible clues to the origins of anomalous or erroneous readings in their texts. Both contain errors arising from inadvertence, and both make use of contractions and suspensions, not all of which are unambiguous. Unusual vocabulary, especially foreign or unfamiliar names, stands out from the scribal transcript as a class of words peculiarly liable to distortion resulting from incomprehension and the resultant reliance on literalism. It is not hard to find comparable examples in print, especially when names occur in the earliest pages set by a given compositor. Thus Compositor D in the Shakespeare First Folio, setting his first pages in *As You Like It* (Q4v-5), gives its heroine's name as "*Rosaline*," a spelling never given by the other two compositors in the play, B and C, but resulting from one of the most common of all confusions to which English secretary hand is liable, that of *e* and *d*, particularly in final position. In the pseudo-Shakespearian *The London Prodigal* (1605),[19] Thomas Creede's compositors similarly misspell two names when they first meet them,

---

[19]Line references are to *The Shakespeare Apocrypha*, ed. C.F. Tucker Brooke (Oxford, 1908).

giving *"Spurrock"* for *"Spurcock"* (*c/r* misreading) on A3
(I.i.108) and "Green-shood" for "Green-sheld" (*o/e* and
o/l) on B3 (II.i.0.1). Later confusions between the speech
prefixes for Sir Arthur Greenshield, *"Arth.,"* and the servant Artychoke, *"Arty.,"* reveal a further detail of the
copy-hand by their confusion of *h* and *y* (and incidentally
reveal that the speech prefixes were in a secretary hand,
in which the confusion is easy, not, as often in scribal
manuscripts, in an Italian hand, in which it is virtually
impossible). Classical and unfamiliar words take a heavy
beating in Creede's 1595 quarto of *Locrine*, whose thirteen
surviving copies give no evidence of stop-press correction,
and equally clear examples are to be found in the anonymous *Reign of King Edward III* (1596), probably printed
by Thomas Scarlet. There misreadings indicate several
confusions of letters, for example that of *y* with *g* in
"Lorragne" for *"Lorrayne"* (A3v: I.i.54.1) and "Crotag"
for "Crotay" (Flv: III.iii.20), or those of *f* and long *s*
combined with *u* and *n* in "Harslen" for "Harfleu" (III.iii.
20). Minim misreadings account for the notorious line
(D4v: II.ii.156) "But I will throng a hellie spout of bloud,"
which aroused Swinburne to an ecstasy of derision, mis-
directed at the unknown author rather than at the compositor who did not recognize that allusions to Hero and
Leander often involve mention of the Hellespont and so
failed to set "But I will through a hellespont of bloud"
correctly. The collection and comparison of all such
errors in a text will enable an editor to identify some of
the letter-forms or combinations in the lost copy which
gave the compositor trouble (even if he may not yet have
identified that compositor) and which may accordingly,
in some cases, help him to identify less obvious corruption.

Indeed, it may generally be worthwhile for the editor
of a printed text to compile as complete a list as he can of

the readings in his text which he has reason to believe in any sense "erroneous or doubtful." Such a list should also contain all those minor mechanical errors or anomalies which it is increasingly the practice even of "critical old-spelling" editors to correct without note, as well as all the variants from the uncorrected states of formes corrected at press. Such lists have long been a feature of the Malone Society's reprints of printed texts, but whether or not it is thought appropriate to publish them, they are of great potential value to any editor examining his text in order to ascertain the extent and nature of the corruption it has suffered in transmission, even through the single stage of translation from manuscript to print. This material may perhaps be thought of as valuable industrial waste, to be recycled by being made available for the scrutiny of all concerned to establish exactly the kinds of error that most easily arose in the Elizabethan printing-house.

That the systematic quantitative and qualitative analysis of the certain or probable errors in every text will always lead to immediate positive results in the detection and cure of less obvious corruption is hardly to be expected, but that such analysis is at least an important approach to the tasks of examination and emendation of the text (which, where a single witness is his sole authority, remain the editor's main responsibility), can be asserted without fear of controversy. Such analysis is also likely both to aid and to be helped by the progressing work of compositor discrimination. It is an approach which few editors, even of the best-known texts, seem to have accepted as a normal part of their editorial strategy: it is also a task within the competence of every editor with access to the mere text he is working with, once he has established the facts ascertainable about that text from the copies in which it is preserved, and from the earliest reprints of it. His findings may include some evidence for a compositor identification, but even if they do not, he will have made a permanent contribution to the understanding of his text and its transmission if he first accurately lists and then classifies in relation to their possible or likely sources the total number of certain or probable errors in that text. This may also prove a safer guide to the detection of further error than those merely statistical estimates of the frequency of error of various kinds in the work of a given compositor which have gained an unfortunate currency among analysts of type-setting since Alice Walker launched them in the mid-1950s. No man is a machine and some generating causes of human error are sporadic. Anyone who has ever read proof of a demanding text hand-set by a highly skilled compositor knows that the frequency of error fluctuates in relation to the relative alertness or weariness of the compositor; at the first onset of tiredness errors may suddenly occur in a cluster, often after pages of impeccable accuracy. The presence of one error may therefore sometimes be the signpost for more. It is, of course, increasingly clear that the job of setting Elizabethan plays in type was not always given to the most highly skilled workmen in the shop (my own candidate for the increasingly popular bibliographical parlour-game of "spot the prentice" being the compositor who set most of Richard Bradock's 1608 quarto of *A Yorkshire Tragedy*). Plays, accordingly, may contain a higher proportion of unsophisticated and clumsy error than many other printed texts—a fact which we are perhaps in danger of losing sight of under the influence of the new conservatism in editing. It is perhaps time that some patient and hard-headed researcher resumed a project outlined and sketchily begun by Halliwell-Phillipps, who had privately printed at Brighton in 1887 a *Dictionary of the Misprints Found in Printed Books of the Sixteenth and Seventeenth Centuries*. This curious work, based on the errata slips of printed books of the period covered, is of only limited value, as it merely lists misreadings, in modern spelling, in parallel with the words which should have been set, and makes no detailed reference to the sources drawn on. Some of the examples are picturesque—*Ile starte thence poore* for *Ile starve their poore*—others familiar, but part of the book's interest resides in the brief comments of a scholar of long and wide experience on the classes of error most commonly to be encountered in printed books of the period: these occur "in final and initial letters, in omissions, in numerals, and in verbal transpositions; but unquestionably the most frequent [are] in pronouns, articles, conjunctions and prepositions" (p.92).

What above all I am urging is the view that the current state of editing is one in which there is some risk of loss of editorial responsibility and alertness, such as is almost bound to arise in the frequent situation where the job does indeed involve mainly the reproduction, literatim and punctuatim, of the text of one early witness. Although this is in itself a more demanding assignment than might be supposed by those who have not attempted it, it can never be assumed that an unthinking conservatism is the right editorial position, nor even a particularly safe one. It may be preferable to uncontrolled eclecticism which does not even accept the responsibility of offering reasoned defence of its decisions, such as characterized many eighteenth- and even nineteenth-century editions of Elizabethan plays, but it falls short of paying the authors of the plays the compliment of assuming that they knew their own language and their chosen profession and of taking their plays seriously enough to verify that these are cleansed of whatever reason can identify as most likely not to represent what they wrote.

Two examples, small enough, but indicative of the danger to which I refer, may help me to cover my retreat and serve as some defence against the charge of labouring the obvious and flogging a whole team of dead horses. They will simultaneously reiterate the need for interrelation between bibliographical research and the study of manuscripts.

In *As You Like It*, the final pairing-off of the lovers takes place under the supervision of the god Hymen, who first presents Rosalind to her father, the exiled Duke, with the lines,

> *Good Duke receiue thy daughter,*
> *Hymen from Heauen brought her,*
> *Yea brought her hether.*
> *That thou mightst ioyne his hand with his,*
> *Whose heart within his bosome is.*
>
> (Slv: TLN 2686-90)

The New Arden editor of the play, Agnes Latham,[20] follows Malone's emendation of the penultimate line to read "join *her* hand with his," but not his continuation of the change into the following line, to give "Whose heart within *her* bosom is." Retaining the Folio's *"his,"* the editor notes that "the F reading *his*, in the first line of the couplet, is pretty clearly a misreading of *hjr*" and adds that "Malone's belief that a similar misreading has affected the second line of the couplet has additional support from the argument of euphony." What might appear a yet stronger argument in support of the double misreading, and of accepting both emendations, is that Compositor B, who set this passage, certainly introduced the misreading of *"his"* for *"hir"* at line 1343, *"Helens cheeke, but not his heart,"* which he read out of context, as it was the first line of another of his pages in the play, R2v. Little reason remains for retaining *"his bosome."*

In the 1594 edition of Marlowe's *Edward II*, which

[20]*As You Like It* (London, 1975).

Fredson Bowers has shown to be the true first edition, set, as he believes, from a manuscript in Marlowe's own hand, two compositors shared the setting, the first (X) setting five gatherings from the beginning of the play, the second (Y) completing it by setting the last seven gatherings. Compositor Y misread a number of proper names, among them *"Levune,"* which he set consistently (and unmetrically) as *"Lewne,"* understandably misreading the unusual medial combination of *vu* as *w*. In his edition (Cambridge, 1973) of Marlowe, Bowers corrects throughout to *"Levune."* Y also provides a variant on the usual form of the name of Sir Thomas Berkeley, one of the keepers of Edward in his captivity, whom he calls *"Bartley."* Bowers, alone among recent editors of *Edward II,* retains this form, without comment, presumably on the assumption that Marlowe had chosen to vary it, though such variation may strike our ears as more extreme than, say, his *"Matrevis"* for "Maltravers," where the consonants remain the same. That Bowers has retained a compositorial misreading cannot be demonstrated beyond question, but Y's other error, combined with the frequency with which Elizabethan compositors confused *t* with *c* or *k*, is enough to give very good general grounds for making the obvious emendation to *"Barcley"* or *"Barkley."*

These examples, from editions which represent the real merits of two current styles of editing, may recommend the view that compositor analysis and the study of Elizabethan manuscripts must remain complementary disciplines, and suggest how the neglect of either may leave editors short of some of the evidence available to help them in deciding about a particular reading.

The familiar point which I have tried to reassert is that in editing every decision about a particular reading must in the end be taken on its own, although in the context of a general hypothesis, and that general considerations relating to the normal classes of error experienced in manuscripts and printed texts of the period are as important a part of the editorial context as are considerations resulting from the detailed study of the transmission of a particular text. There may be printed plays of the Elizabethan period which do not contain unambiguous indications of the general character of the manuscripts from which they were printed, whether authorial or scribal, foul papers or fair copy, prompt-book or author's papers annotated in preparation for the transcription of the prompt-book; there can hardly be any which do not contain indications of some physical details of those lost manuscripts, in the form of spellings, characteristic errors identifiable as result-ing from misreading, formal matters of layout, especially of non-textual matter, act and scene headings, stage direc-tions and speech prefixes. I think it possible—and this is my main contention—that the history of textual studies of the Elizabethan drama in the past half-century reveals a growing and by now excessive concentration on matters of sometimes fruitless speculation and on bibliographical techniques which, though indeed of great importance for the final resolution of many large questions about the nature and early transmission of play texts, are of limited practical utility, and on the attempt to codify into unduly rigid categories materials which, by their very nature, can only be distorted by such endeavours.

SHAKESPEARE RESTORED—ONCE AGAIN!

G. Blakemore Evans

I have taken the first part of my title from what may fairly be described as the earliest book devoted to the textual criticism of Shakespeare—Lewis Theobald's *Shakespeare Restored* published in 1726—a textual onslaught on Pope's edition of Shakespeare's plays that was to earn for Theobald ("pidling Tibald" as Pope dubbed him)· his uneasy eminence as the first hero of *The Dunciad*. Theobald's title reflects, of course, his desire to castigate Pope as editor, but it also suggests something of an eighteenth-century optimism about the concept and possible extent of restoration, through emendation and eclecticism, that modern successors in the long line of Shakespearean editors would hesitate to claim. We know, to be sure, a great deal more than did Theobald about the whole textual situation, but ironically, because we do know so much more, we also know that only to a limited extent can Shakespeare's text ever be "restored." Nonetheless, some vestige of that optimism lingers, calling editors from the "vasty deep," and despite doubters like Hotspur they continue to come in an attempt to alleviate in some small way the "dram of ev'l" that "Doth all the noble substance often dout" (as Steevens did, rightly or wrongly, in this famous crux in *Hamlet*). It is in connection with the most recent of these attempts, *The Riverside Shakespeare*,[1] on which I worked as textual editor, that I have been asked to say something today.

---

[1] *The Riverside Shakespeare*, eds. G. Blakemore Evans, Harry Levin, Herschel Baker, Anne Barton, Frank Kermode, Hallett Smith, Marie Edel (Boston, 1974).

"It is," says Cowley, "a hard and nice Subject for a Man to write of himself," and I apologize to begin with for the unseemly number of first person pronouns that dot the following comments. The editing of Shakespeare's complete works had occupied my mind and been a kind of dream long before I finally undertook, in 1960, what Pope called the "dull duty." While I was still an undergraduate, my father, who had himself devoted long years to an edition of the Lucerne Passion Play, gave me a number of books that had belonged to a cousin of my mother's, W.J. Craig, the editor of the often reprinted *Oxford Shakespeare*. Among them were the earlier volumes of Hazlitt's *Dodsley* and Thomas Hawkins' *The Origin of the English Drama* (the latter a gift to Craig from Edward Dowden), all filled with Craig's almost illegible and sometimes rude annotations (he had a low opinion of W.C. Hazlitt). Thus, both by heredity and by example, one might say, adapting Cowley's comment on his own early exposure to Spenser, I "was made an [editor] as irremediably as a Child is made an Eunuch"—an analogy I would dare allow myself only in a gathering of fellow editors!

Although the editing of a modernized text of the complete works differs more in quantity than in kind from the editing of single plays in the canon, the sheer weight of such quantity (thirty-eight plays, the *More* passages, and the poems and sonnets) makes it imperative for an editor to decide at the earliest possible stage what kind of overall text he wishes to offer and then to evolve a set of editorial decisions that may be applied consistently throughout the whole corpus. Herein lies one of the principal difficulties. Whereas the little-minded hobgoblin Consistency is troublesome enough within the limits of a single play, give him the field and he becomes a roaring devil. I was, of course, immeasurably aided in this particular battle by Marvin Spevack's monumental and invaluable six-volume *Concordance*, which, since it was prepared from galleys of the *Riverside* text, was available to me in print-outs during the later stages of my work, making innumerable small adjustments possible.

My textual policies are set out at length in the *Riverside* edition and there would be little point in restating them here. General principles are usually pretty dull tools to talk about unless one has the fun of applying them. Instead, I would like, with an occasional inevitable glance at policy, to discuss certain specific matters that confront all editors of Shakespeare from time to time, but of which an editor becomes more widely conscious when he looks at the Shakespeare canon as a whole.

One of these—to adopt W.J. Bate's phrase—is what I may call "the burden of the past." This "burden" has several faces. Its weight is felt, most noticeably perhaps, in the immense amount of past editorial labor that has been lavished, occasionally wantonly, but more often both significantly and influentially, on Shakespeare's plays and poems. Any editor of a classic English text bears this burden to some extent, but with Shakespeare one must reckon with not perhaps five or six predecessors but with more than thirty earlier editors of the complete works (many of them producing several revised editions), not to mention the veritable army of editors who have multiplied editions, often important, of single plays, and the innumerable, frequently amateur, emenders whose happy thoughts, mostly wild but sometimes inspired, litter the textual notes of a variorum edition.

No one, of course, would be foolish enough to wish this vast body of editorial work undone, and any editor of Shakespeare profits immeasurably from the labors of his predecessors, particularly from the work of certain individuals: Rowe (partly because he was the first in the field), Theobald, Capell, Malone, Dyce, Wright, Dover Wilson,

Kittredge, and Alexander, men whom the modern editor quickly comes to recognize as giants in the tradition. Nevertheless, in a sense this is the burden. It is often difficult for an editor to look with fresh, unblinkered eyes on a textual crux, the solution of which has been given the benediction of many years of editorial unanimity by his elders and (often) his betters.

Let me offer two examples, the first one of the most famous of all emendations—Theobald's "'a babbl'd of green fields" in *Henry V* (II.iii.16-17). It has since been argued, with some justification, that, given the special characteristics of the secretary hand, the Folio reading "a table of greene fields" is more likely to be a compositor's misreading of his manuscript copy's "a talkd of greene fields." Interestingly enough, this was the reading first suggested to Theobald by an anonymous gentleman, on the basis of which Theobald was led to his celebrated "'a babbl'd," a debt he acknowledged in *Shakespeare Restored* but failed to acknowledge, alas, in his slightly later edition. It has, moreover, been questioned whether any emendation at all is required, taking the Folio "table" in the sense of picture and "greene fields" as a careless reading for Greenfield's or Grenville's (i.e., Sir Richard Grenville of *Revenge* renown)—a suggestion I find little more appealing than Pope's invention of a propertyman called Greenfield, whose prompt note, calling for a table, he suggested had been wrongly incorporated into the text. The weight of tradition is heavily against abandoning Theobald's reading, and editions, including my own, continue to perpetuate what may well be only Theobald's inspired improvement of a comparatively flat authorial "talk'd."

A similar pressure may perhaps be seen at work in a famous passage in *Macbeth* (II.ii. 58-60), where our only substantive text (the First Folio) reads: "no: this my

Hand will rather / The multitudinous Seas incarnardine, /
Making the Greene one, Red." The comma after "one"
first dropped out in the 1673 quarto and the Fourth Folio
(1685), but it is not clear how early editors like Rowe,
Theobald, or Warburton, who also dropped the comma,
understood the passage, though Garrick, in his earlier
career, is reported to have spoken the final half-line with
an emphasis that conveyed the sense of making a green
sea, a red sea (i.e., following what in fact seems to be the
force of the Folio pointing). Johnson was probably the
earliest editor to attempt an emendation in the spirit of
the copy-text (Pope's ugly botch, followed by the obse-
quious Hanmer, omits "The multitudinous Seas incarnardine," and reads " . . . no, this my hand will rather / Make
the green ocean red—" a characteristic example of Pope's
butcherly editing). Johnson pointed the line as "Making
the green, One red—", treating it, like Pope, as broken off
by Lady Macbeth's entry and implying "sea" or "ocean"
to complete it. Finally, Arthur Murphy suggested the
reading first adopted by Steevens, by proposing "Making
the green—one red" (i.e., turning the natural green of the
seas uniformly red). Murphy's interpretation has a strong
imaginative suggestiveness, but there are difficulties.
Shakespeare, among his 1,943 other uses of "one," no-
where applies it in exactly this sense (i.e., total, or uniform), his nearest approach being the phrase "all one."
In other words, it would seem that Shakespeare would
have been more likely to write "Making the green all one
red." Malone denounced Murphy's reading as semantically
un-Elizabethan and for the first time restored the Folio
pointing. Nor is the *OED* helpful, failing to cite the
Macbeth passage and offering no others significantly
analogous. Murphy's reading has indeed been defended by
reference to Percy Simpson's demonstration, in *Shakespeare's Punctuation*, that a comma was sometimes used

following a word to indicate emphasis, but Simpson does not cite this example, and the capitalization of both "Greene" and "Red" in the Folio would seem (also according to Simpson) to throw the emphasis on those two words and not on "one." Most recent editors, except Dover Wilson, who follows Murphy's pointing, take advantage of modern punctuation and omit the First Folio comma after "one," producing a reading that is ambiguous and may be read either way. Nevertheless, they all interpret the line in Murphy's sense and usually suggest no alternative meaning. Thus, once again, an editor must determine whether he is "restoring" Shakespeare or "improving" him, and whether an earlier editorial decision, based largely on esthetic considerations, should outweigh the rather unsatisfactory evidence of linguistic usage and what appears to be the clear intent of the First Folio pointing. I must plead guilty, if that is the right word, to once more following the crowd.

A second aspect of the burden of the past—a kind of counter-reaction to the first—is the temptation to break with earlier editorial tradition and to rescue an almost universally rejected copy-text reading from the oblivion which, perhaps, it deserves. It is a sweet temptation, since it partakes of the very essence of restoration, but like emendation it has its obvious dangers. The kinds of arguments just advanced against Murphy's emendation in *Macbeth*, in favor of the First Folio pointing of the passage, may indicate something of the problem involved. Sometimes, however, yielding to this temptation has produced happy results. Obvious examples would be such restorations as Percy Simpson's "pair-taunt-like" in *Love's Labor's Lost* (V.ii.67), Duthie-Wilson's "niesse" from Q2 "Neece" in *Romeo and Juliet* (II.ii.167) for the usual Q4 "dear" (itself an attempt at emendation), Chambers' (following Ulrici) "a rose, / By any other word," also from

Q2 of *Romeo and Juliet* (II.ii.44), for the "bad" quarto's "other name," and Dover Wilson's (following an anonymous conjecture) "sallied / sullied flesh" from Q2 of *Hamlet* (I.ii.129) for the flat "solid Flesh" of the First Folio. The last two restorations illustrate one of the problems faced by an editor: the difficulty of substituting a new reading, however authoritative, for one that has become enshrined in the popular memory. Hamlet's "solid flesh" and Juliet's "a rose by any other name" still remain as clarion calls to combat for many readers.

Like most editors, I have, though with some trepidation, added my small quota to such retrievals, and, at the risk of incurring instant annihilation, I will offer here some examples: in *Lear* (IV.i.10), "My father, parti-ey'd?" (with the meaning "motley-eyed") from the corrected state of Q1 ("parti, eyd") for the usual F1 "poorely led" (deriving from the uncorrected state of Q1 ["poorlie, leed"]); in *Hamlet* (IV.vii.171), "cull-cold" (with the sense "chaste") from Q2 in place of the F1 "cold;" in *Coriolanus* (IV.vii.55), "Rights by rights fouler" (i.e., rights made less fair by other rights) for Malone's commonly accepted emendation of F1 "fouler" to "falter;" in *Troilus and Cressida* (I.iii.55), "Thou great commander, nerves and bone of Greece," where past editors have chosen the F1 "nerve," although the Q reading is supported by a line in V.viii.12: "Here lies thy heart, thy sinews, and thy bone" (common to both Q and F1); and in *II Henry IV* (IV.iv.32), "Open as day for meting charity" (i.e., dealing out charity) from the Q "meeting" for the commonly accepted F1 "melting" ("meting," it may be noted, accords better with "Open" than "melting").

Sometimes an editor, contemplating the possibility of restoration, may decide that "the better part of valor is discretion" (the phrase may very often be interpreted in Falstaff's sense), as I have already indicated in earlier discussion of the passage from *Macbeth*. But two other examples of my "discretion" may perhaps be worth noticing. I wrestled long and hard with the F1 reading of the following lines from *The Comedy of Errors* (I.ii.4): "This very day a *Syracusian* Marchant / Is apprehended for a riuall here," where "a riuall" (in the slightly extended sense of "an enemy") is emended to "arrivall" in F2, the reading followed in all subsequent editions. What made me hesitate here, when I was willing to take the plunge on other restorations? The slightly wrenched meaning required for "riuall," the spectre of a mere dropped "r" in F1, or the burden of editorial tradition? I am not sure, perhaps all three. At any rate, the best I could muster was a textual note suggesting the possibility of the F1 reading. The second and better-known case occurs in *Richard III* (V.iii.183), where Q1 (here the copy-text) reads: "Richard loues Richard, that is I and I." This was changed in Q2 to "Richard loues Richard, that is I am I," picked up in F1, and accepted by editors ever since. Malone first noted the Q1 reading and, though he did not adopt it, said that he was "not sure that it is not right." It should also be observed that the Q2 reading ("I am I") could very easily be the result of compositorial eye-slip since the following line ends with "I am" (a kind of argument that is often invoked to support an emendation or restoration). Nevertheless, I hewed to the traditional line and again satisfied my conscience with a special textual note. Someday, perhaps, an editor will have the courage or the foolhardiness, whichever it may be, to adopt one or both of these readings.

The burden of the past has operated most generally, however, in two larger areas: the leveling and modernization of certain characteristic Elizabethan-Jacobean spellings which reflect, or may reflect, regular contemporary pronunciation or variant pronunciations of the same word; and the imposition on the text of a uniform, modern, and more or less logical system of punctuation. Both movements were essentially accomplished by the eighteenth-century editors, and modern editors, with a few exceptions (notably, Dover Wilson and Sisson in the handling of the pointing of the early texts, and Kittredge and J.C. Maxwell [in his New Arden *Titus Andronicus*] in the retention of selected Elizabethan-Jacobean spelling forms), have pretty much followed the traditional paths laid down by the eighteenth century and given the seal of approval by the old standard Globe text. The *Riverside* text breaks with tradition in both these matters.

The problem of characteristic spelling forms may be illustrated, first, by examining Shakespeare's use of proper or place names. If Shakespeare and his contemporaries talked about Callice, Harflew, Roan, Rossillion, Joan de Pucelle or Joan of Aire, Britains, and Bullingbrook, for example, with what propriety does a modern text turn these into Calais, Harfleur, Rouen, Rousillon, Joan la Pucelle or Joan of Arc, Bretons, and Bolingbroke? Why should we read "Dauphin" when Shakespeare regularly wrote "Dolphin," or "Birnam Wood" when F1 nine out of ten times spells it "Birnan" or "Birnane" and is supported in the final "n" form by Holinshed and other early historians? With what may be called "common" words the same questions may also be asked. Shakespeare always uses such ordinal forms as "fift," "sixt," "eight," "twelf," and "twentith." Are we not doing violence to his language to convert these into "fifth," "sixth," etc.? Or should the contemporary diversity of such variant forms as "perfit" and "perfect," "bankrout" and "bankrupt," "conster" and "construe," "tenure" and "tenor," "commandement" and "commandment," "wrastle" and "wrestle," "ruffin" and "ruffian," "randon" and "random," "fadom" and "fathom," "terrestial" and "terrestrial" be sacrificed to achieve a simplistic and un-

Elizabethan uniformity? I for one do not believe that the lively and Protean variety of Elizabethan English should be submerged in this way and I have gone further than others, though selectively, in attempting to preserve it, realizing at the same time, of course, that I am treading (delicately, I trust) on highly controversial ground.

Before turning to the problem of punctuation, referred to above, I would like to call attention to another aspect of Elizabethan spelling that may on occasion raise substantive difficulties for an editor: the use of a common single spelling form for words of different meaning; for example, "loose" (meaning *lose* or *loose*), "humaine" (meaning *human* or *humane*), capital "I" (i.e., the first-person pronoun or *ay* meaning *yes*), "then" (meaning *then* or *than*), "travel" (meaning *travail* or *travel*), "borne" (meaning *born* or *borne*), "least" (meaning *lest* or *least*), and the relatively infrequent "of" (meaning *off* or *of*). The well-known "shard-borne Beetle" crux in *Macbeth* (III.ii.41-43) offers an obvious example of the problem such common spellings can pose for an editor, since "shard-borne" can be interpreted either way (i.e., borne aloft on scaly wings, or, without the final "e," born [i.e., generated] in cow dung). A similar difficulty arises in *Love's Labor's Lost* (I.i.172) with what are described in the copy-text as Armado's "high-borne words," which editors up to now have regularly read as "high-born," following F3. "High-borne," however, in the sense of "lofty," better fits the character of Armado and is echoed a few lines later (1.193) in Berowne's reference to his "high words." The "I/ay" confusion may be neatly illustrated by some lines in *Timon of Athens* (IV.iii.477-78), which in F1 read: "I neuer had honest man about me, I all / I kept were Knaues, ..." Most editions since Capell's, including my own, point the lines as follows: "I never had honest man about me, I; all / I kept were knaves, ..."

Delius, however, approximating more closely to the F1 pointing, proposed the perhaps more rhythmically natural reading: "I never had honest man about me. Ay, all / I kept were knaves, ..." Second thoughts suggest I should probably have followed Delius. One further example: the "least/lest" ambiguity. Lines 128-29 of V.iii in *The Winter's Tale* read in F1: "There's time enough for that, / Least they desire (vpon this push) to trouble / Your ioys, with like relation." Although all editions since F3 have hitherto interpreted the F1 "Least" as "Lest" (usually without a textual note), I decided to retain "Least," since, with a semi-colon after "that" (as in F2), I believe it makes superior sense (i.e., the last thing they [Florizel and Perdita] wish at this time of emotional crisis is to disturb your happiness by a similar account). The point, here, however, is that either reading is possible, and an editor owes it to his reader to admit the presence of such ambiguity in a textual or glossarial note.

I will return now to the problems posed by Elizabethan-Jacobean punctuation. The subject is a somewhat controversial one, as we have seen in the passage from *Macbeth* ("Making the Greene one, Red") discussed earlier: controversial both in terms of how certain marks of punctuation are to be interpreted and in terms of the authority of the early punctuation—whether authorial or for the most part compositorial. On the second matter, for example, does the comparatively light pointing of the early quartos reflect Shakespeare's preference (when he bothered to punctuate, which, on the evidence of the *Sir Thomas More* scene, if we accept it as being in his hand, seems to have been almost not at all), or does it merely reflect printing-house practice that, by the time of the First Folio, was to become noticeably heavier? Admitting all the imponderables and uncertainties, I very early decided to give as much weight as was reasonable in a modernized text to the special characteristics of the punctuation in each of the chosen copy-texts. If not Shakespeare's, it was at least the work of his contemporaries, men in whom the rhythms and special emphases of his language were alive and immediately felt. By a policy of selective modernization I believed I was able to retain something of the fluidity and cohesiveness of the original without imposing on the text as a whole either a merely antiquarian faithfulness or the Iron Maiden of modern logical punctuation.

Certain idiosyncrasies of Elizabethan-Jacobean punctuation offer special difficulties or ambiguities. Among them, I would like to illustrate two: the omission of some kind of necessary pointing, and the use of the comma between phrases or clauses in a way that leaves their correct relationship uncertain. The resulting ambiguities may call for editorial decisions that are in fact quite arbitrary, and editors often fail to indicate in their textual notes or elsewhere that such an editorial decision has been imposed on the text. An example from *II Henry IV* (I.ii.12-19) will serve to illustrate both lack of punctuation and the use of the all-purpose comma. The quarto copy-text reads: "if the prince put thee into my seruice for any other reason then to sett me off, why then I haue no iudgement thou horeson mandrake, thou art fitter to be worne in my cap, then to wait at my heels I was neuer man- /ned with an agot till now, but I wil in-set you, neither in golde nor siluer, but in vile apparell, and send you backe againe to your master for a iewell, ..." The question which teases an editor in this passage is, of course, where the phrase "thou horeson mandrake" belongs. Does it go with "why then I haue no iudgement [,] thou horeson mandrake [.]," as the Q comma and earlier lack of punctuation would seem to indicate and where it serves as a natural complement to the phrase "to sett me off," or does it open the next sentence, "Thou hòreson mandrake, thou art fitter to be worne in my cap," etc.? The Fl text chooses the second alternative, placing a period after "iudgement" and retaining the Q comma after "mandrake," and has been followed by all editors. The influence of the pointing in other early texts, in this case Fl, is always, and naturally, strong, but since the first alternative makes equally good (perhaps even better) sense and the pointing in the other early text is most often nothing more authoritative than one man's guess, an editor should at least warn the reader by a textual note that the copy-text has been emended and thus give him the opportunity to make his own judgment on the evidence.

A more complex example of what may be called the Elizabethan "comma fault" occurs in a speech of Constance's in *King John* (III.i.108-9), where our only substantive text, the First Folio, reads:

> Arme, arme, you heauens, against these periur'd Kings,
> A widdow cries, be husband to me (heauens)

Apart from the final parenthetical "(heauens)," the lines are pointed throughout with commas, leaving an editor with three possible choices. He may read:

> Arm, arm, you heavens, against these perjur'd kings!
> A widow cries, be husband to me, heavens!

or

> Arm, arm, you heavens! Against these perjur'd kings
> A widow cries. Be husband to me, heavens!

or

> Arm, arm, you heavens, against these perjur'd kings!
> A widow cries; be husband to me, heavens!

There is in each of these three readings a slight but significant difference, but the editor can choose only one. Without proper textual annotation, therefore, his final text will seem much more authoritative than it actually is.

I have already touched on some of the problems raised by emendation. The urge to leave "Bill Stumps his mark" on the text, what might in other words be described as the "Warburton syndrome," is strong and humanly very understandable. I do not have time to pursue the more fascinating aberrations of the topic here, but there is one fairly recent development, emendation based on compositor study, that should perhaps be briefly noted, if only by way of admonition. The practice has emerged largely through the valuable compositor studies of Alice Walker and Charlton Hinman and, therefore, carries with it some aura of "scientific" bibliography. Roughly stated, the theory argues (1) that because a compositor may be shown as liable to various kinds of error or sophistication in one place, he is likely to be guilty of similar errors or sophistications in other passages also set by him, and (2) that on the basis of this possibility an editor has the right to emend such passages, if they pose any irregularity or seeming difficulty, in the light of that compositor's supposedly known errant proclivities. This is an unfriendly, and some might say an unfair, statement of the theory, and I will plead guilty to being unfriendly at least, because I think such an approach to the copy-text is in general highly subjective, despite its appearance of scientific method, and dangerously meddling, threatening what E.A.J. Honigmann, who takes a similarly dim view, calls "the stability of Shakespeare's text"—a text which we now know is unstable enough in the first place.

The preceding criticism leads me to my final point— the status of the principle of copy-text. Once having determined on the copy-text, how far is an editor a master or a slave? Eighteenth- and nineteenth-century editors, with the partial exception of Capell, were not overly exercised by this matter and were, generally speaking, heartily eclectic. Today, however, an editor has to face the question. My own view is that the editor is neither master nor slave and that, while he should always allow special weight to the authority of the copy-text, he should do so without permitting himself to be tyrannized by it. The problem in this instance is not primarily one of emendation of copy-text readings that are, or appear to be, corrupt. That aspect we have touched on earlier and it is my firm conviction that in this area an editor should meddle and make as little as possible. But, in the case of two- or three-text plays, the copy-text is open to a form of emendation in at least two other ways, namely, when other early texts supply words, lines, or passages lacking in the copy-text or when they offer variant readings that may seem especially appealing to an editor. Both these forms of emendation, particularly the second, open the door to the danger of more or less unprincipled eclecticism in terms of the principle of copy-text.

Usually there is substantial agreement among editors about admitting to the received text such lines or passages as they conceive to be authorial, even when such a procedure produces a final text, as in the case of *Hamlet*, probably never read or seen by Shakespeare or his contemporaries. Occasionally, however, particularly when the additional material is drawn from an early text of questionable authority, such as a "bad" quarto, questions may arise. Let me cite one such case in which I decided to fly in the face of editorial tradition. In Q1 of *King Lear*, a memorially contaminated text, as Edmund is belatedly trying to do "some good . . . despite of mine own nature," we read: "*Edg.* To who my Lord, who hath the office, send / Thy token of repreeue. / *Bast.* Well thought on, take my sword, the Captaine, / Giue it the Captaine?" (V.iii.251). Almost all editors follow F1 (the copy-text) and Q2 in omitting "the Captaine" after "take my sword" and they may, of course, be right. But there is, I believe, sufficient justification for retaining the Q1 addition. The two words ("the Captaine") complete metrically what is otherwise a four-stress line; and, in context, pointed with a period after "sword" and a dash after "Captaine," they help through dramatic broken syntax to stress Edmund's exhausted state of mind ("Well thought on. Take my sword. The Captain– / Give it the Captain."). Moreover, it is possible, given the confused textual situation in *Lear* generally, and particularly in the last act, that the F1 omission was influenced by the similar omission in Q2, and that Q2, since sheets I and L in Q1 have survived in only one state, was printed from a state of sheet L (either corrected or uncorrected) which omitted the words.

These seemed to me sound reasons for accepting the Q1 addition into the received text; to other editors, who doubtless considered the same evidence, they did not. Herein, of course, lies the life blood which keeps the editing and re-editing of Shakespeare a viable and exciting pursuit–the opportunity it still affords the editor, despite what I have called the "burden of the past" (in part, indeed, even because of it) and all the numerous advances of modern analytical bibliography, to exercise his own critical judgment and taste, good or bad.

The second form of emendation mentioned above, that is the substitution of a seemingly preferable variant from another substantive or semi-substantive text for the reading of the copy-text, poses a larger threat to the principle of copy-text. Much depends, of course, on the presumed authority and provenience of the copy-text. The comparatively uncertain textual situation in *Othello*, for example, necessitates adopting a different attitude to the F1 copy-text than an editor would ordinarily take where the authority of the copy-text was clearer, as, let us say, in *I Henry IV*. Nevertheless, even in *Othello*, where my text admits roughly 190 readings from Q1, most of them, of course, either restored oaths or necessary corrections, it is, I believe, the duty of an editor to hold closely to the F1 copy-text unless significant reasons can be offered for substituting a reading from Q1. It is not acceptable, it seems to me, to substitute one more or less indifferent reading for another on the basis of what really amounts to no more than personal whim. There is, for example, no sound reason that I can see for reading "I warrant it grieves my husband / As if the case were his" (III.iii.3-4), thus adopting the Q1 "case" for the copy-text "cause." That at least two important recent texts of *Othello* so read underlines my concern for the principle of copy-text.

Let me conclude with a sad example of the opposite extreme—uncritical adherence to the copy-text. Some lines from Hamlet's address to the Ghost (I.iv.48-51) read as follows in the Q2 copy-text: ". . . why the Sepulcher, / Wherein we saw thee quietly interr'd / Hath op't his ponderous and marble iawes, / To cast thee vp againe?" The F1 text agrees exactly, except for one word. In place of "interr'd" it reads "enurn'd," a reading accepted by all editors even since Dover Wilson established Q2 as the basic copy-text. The arguments for preferring F1 "enurn'd" to "interr'd" are several. Since Act 1 in Q2 is generally believed to be strongly influenced by, if not indeed printed from, a corrected copy of Q1 (a "bad" quarto), its readings are open to suspicion, even though there is evidence, as elsewhere in this speech, of correction in Q2 from an independent manuscript, almost certainly Shakespeare's "foul papers." Moreover, though it is possible that Shakespeare originally wrote "interr'd," it is highly unlikely that anyone but Shakespeare would have substituted a neologism like "enurn'd" (in the peculiarly Shakespearean sense of "buried") for a comparatively commonplace word that more obviously fitted the general context. In fact, the process usually works in the other direction, where, as in *King Lear*, rare or unusual words like "dearn" (III.vii.63) and "stopple" (V.iii.156), preserved in Q1, were reduced to "stern" and "stop" in the theatrically contaminated F1 copy-text. Why, then, even if Shakespeare originally wrote "interr'd," which on the evidence now seems to me unlikely, and later substituted the more metaphorically powerful "enurn'd," did I retain the relatively colorless Q2 reading? With hindsight, it is clear that I failed in this instance to consider all the evidence, particularly the important status of "enurn'd" as a Shakespearean neologism, and allowed myself to be blinded by an excessive veneration for the principle of copy-text. Too much may be as dangerous as too little.

I end, intentionally, on a note of *peccavi*. No editor of the complete Shakespeare canon, once his labors have been frozen by the cold finality of print, can fail to be conscious of how frequently he has erred and how imperfectly he has realized his brave dream of *Shakespeare Restored*. Thus the slight bitterness of the final exclamation mark in my title is, I suppose, unescapable.

ITALIAN RENAISSANCE PLAYS:
PROBLEMS AND OPPORTUNITIES

Beatrice Corrigan

When I was invited by Dr. Kathleen Speight to prepare a volume of Renaissance plays for the Manchester University Press Italian Texts series, of which she is general editor, we decided on two works, a comedy by Ariosto and a tragedy by Trissino, as representative of the earliest phase of modern European drama. We agreed that I should supply the texts in the form of xeroxes of reliable editions, a procedure which would eliminate typing errors in transcription and which would result in copy that the printers would find easy to follow.

Ariosto's *Il Negromante* presented no difficulties, for his comedies are available in the reliable edition of Michele Catalano (1933), based on printed texts and on manuscripts where they exist. Trissino's *Sofonisba*, however, proved to be a different matter. The first modern regular tragedy, a model for the French classical theatre as well as for the Italian, it has been more frequently reprinted than any other tragedy of the period. As there has been a post-war revival of interest in Renaissance drama, the play is included in three modern Italian anthologies, edited by reputable scholars and issued by reputable publishers. I procured a xerox of the play from one of these anthologies, and sat down, rather casually I am afraid, to collate it with the early editions, two of 1524 and one of 1529, prepared under the author's supervision. I soon became less casual: in the modern edition lines were reversed, lines were omitted, half-lines were omitted, the names of speakers were omitted, with joyous disregard for sense and prosody. The important dedication to Leo X was omitted completely. This proved to be true for all three anthologies. In one, the lines of the play were numbered, but in two places a line had vanished, so that the numbering soon became meaningless.

The punctuation had been mutilated with similar barbarity. Trissino's punctuation is careful, considered, and generally consistent, though he frequently uses a colon followed by a capital letter as an alternative for a full stop —a not uncommon sixteenth-century practice. In the 1529 edition he often substitutes a semicolon for a comma, possibly to indicate a slow, stately utterance in an important speech. Through successive centuries, editors had sprinkled his text liberally with exclamation marks (which he never used), had omitted full stops and commas, had substituted one mark for another: had, in short, committed every enormity of punctuation that accident or intent could engender.

It was during this painful but educational experience that I learned something about the problems of editing Italian Renaissance drama. I must be forgiven if I refer rather frequently in this paper to Ariosto and to Trissino.

Perhaps at this point I should explain the present situation with regard to editions of the Renaissance plays. The various nineteenth-century reprints, with a few exceptions, are unconcerned with accuracy. Early in the twentieth century more professional editing began, and many plays were included in the Scrittori d'Italia series, whose founder, and for many years general editor, was Benedetto Croce. The policy of the series was to present a text based on the most reliable early edition, with some variants and a brief bibliographical introduction, but no explanatory notes. Any of the plays in that series might profitably be re-edited with a little less austerity. Ariosto's comedies were edited by Catalano independently: he indicated textual variants of different editions and manuscripts, but provided no notes. This edition was reissued recently by

Rizzoli; the variants were omitted and some notes explanatory of the text were added. Outstanding modern critical
editions, with text, notes, and introduction, are Roberto
Ridolfi's *Mandragola* (1965), Giorgio Petrocchi's 1971
presentation of all the plays of Aretino, and Florindo
Cerreta's editions of Alessandro Piccolomini's *L'Alessandro* in 1966, and of Scipione Bargagli's *La Pellegrina* (a
source for George Chapman's *May Day*) in 1971. Many
reprints and anthologies published in recent years are no
more reliable than their nineteenth-century forerunners,
as I have already shown.

Some of the problems I am about to mention exist in
editing English and Spanish plays as well, but in the editing
of Italian plays often have a specifically Italian complexity.
One of the difficulties that may be encountered in establishing a text I can illustrate by a quotation from the
prologue of Ariosto's second version of *La Cassaria* (*The
Coffer*). The first version had been performed in Ferrara,
possibly in 1502, certainly in 1508, then not again until
1529, and between then and 1531 Ariosto rewrote the
play, this time in verse. He explains one of his reasons as
follows: "*The Coffer*, which made its debut on this very
stage twenty years ago . . . , pleased everyone. But it did
not receive a worthy reward, for it became the prey of
greedy printers who tore it apart, doing what they liked
with it; then they sold it everywhere—in shops and public
markets—to whomsoever would buy it, at bargain prices."[1]

It is evident then that the first edition of a play published in its author's lifetime can be accepted only with
caution as the basis of a critical text. When Ariosto wrote
his early plays, comedy in the vernacular was such a
novelty that everyone was wild with eagerness to read

---

[1] *The Comedies of Ariosto*, tr. E.A. Beame and L.G. Sbrocchi (Chicago, 1974),
p. 203.

examples of this delightful invention. Printing in Italy had passed through its first uncertain childhood, and was flourishing with almost alarming vigour. New presses sprang up in a score of cities, and printers vied with each other in producing novelties that would sell. The poet often could not resist confiding manuscript copies of his work to his friends, who passed them on, also in confidence, to their friends. Ariosto in a letter accuses the actors in his plays, who were of course his fellow-courtiers, of having given copies to a printer, who cared little for the accuracy or ownership of a text as long as it could find buyers and make him a profit. The first edition of the prose *Cassaria* is without imprint, but was almost certainly printed in Ferrara in 1516-17,[2] possibly in an effort to profit from the publicity surrounding the long-awaited, newly-published *Orlando Furioso*. The play was reprinted twice in 1525, in Rome and in Venice, four years after the second edition of the *Furioso*, and again in Venice in 1526. All these editions fall within Ariosto's lifetime (he died in 1533), yet he had sanctioned none of them. There were four more editions of this pirated version before the end of the century, each probably adding its own misprints to the confusion.

The two earliest editions of *Il Negromante* as well are without imprint, and it is difficult to determine which is the first. Both came out in Venice in 1534, the year after their author's death, and there were two more editions in 1535, both in Venice but by different printers. Catalano himself knew of only one of the anonymous editions, a copy of which he owned. It may be mentioned that in all editions and manuscripts of the first version of this play there is a line missing.

[2]Bibliographical details for Ariosto's plays are taken from G. Agnelli and G. Ravegnani, *Annali delle edizioni ariostee* (Bologna, 1931).

It should not be assumed that successive editors detect and correct the mistakes in their predecessors' texts. On the contrary, grave distrust should be felt for any edition that bears on its title page some such phrase as "reprinted and corrected anew with the greatest diligence." Such a formula means only that the publisher hopes to lure purchasers into buying what they think is a superior edition to the one they already have. For instance, Sofonisba, in line 14 of the 1524 and 1529 editions of Trissino's play, reminds her friend Erminia that they "have been *nutrite* (nurtured) together." In a 1587 edition, which carries the magic guarantee of diligent correction, this has been changed to *nutrice:* they "have been a wet-nurse together." Printers of the period had a philosophical attitude to misprints at the best of times. As one says, "It is human to err, and the mistakes are all of a kind that the intelligent reader can correct for himself."

One test of a reliable edition is a dedication by the author, and any edition earlier than the one bearing a dedication should be regarded with suspicion. Obviously a manuscript copy, unless it is an autograph, has no more authority than a printed text. A holograph may represent the author's final version; but, on the other hand, it may only represent one of his efforts to master an unfamiliar genre. Christina Roaf of Oxford has recently discovered in the Vatican Library an autograph manuscript of Sperone Speroni's *Canace.*[3] It is the basis for the Valgrisi edition of 1546 published in Venice, which is thus established as the authentic text. A pirated Florentine edition of the same year is full of errors. An autograph first draft of the tragedy also exists, was published in 1740, and was

---

[3]"A New Autograph of Sperone Speroni's *Canace*," in *Essays in Honour of John Humphreys Whitfield*, ed. H.C. Davis, D.G. Rees, J.M. Hatwell, G.W. Slowey (London, 1975), pp.137-54.

previously accepted as the authorized version. Only now can a reliable critical text be prepared. Other cases could be cited in which a fairly recent discovery of a manuscript has made possible an authentic text of a well-known play. For example, Ariosto left an unfinished comedy, *Gli Studenti*, which was later completed and published by his brother. It was not until 1915 that the extent of the original work was known, when another completed manuscript version, this time by his son, was found, and by comparison the place where the continuations began could be determined. Also, very recently Professor Cerreta has published an article discussing an autograph manuscript of *La Pellegrina*,[4] discovered too late to be used in his admirable edition of the play but fortunately not affecting its authority as the definitive text.

Giorgio Petrocchi has been fortunate in his edition of Aretino's plays. For many of them the original manuscript still exists, and Aretino generally supervised his first editions but did not trouble to revise, so that it can be assumed that later readings are not by his hand.

A kindred problem is that of locating all the editions of a play. Florindo Cerreta has identified seventeen editions of *Gl'Ingannati* in the sixteenth and seventeenth centuries, and has determined their relationship. He proves that the 1537-38 edition used in 1912 for Sanesi's critical edition was not actually the first edition of the play. Only one copy of the real first edition was known to survive, in a famous Milanese collection, and it perished during the last war.

When the choice of the basic text and the necessary collations have been made, the question of transcription also poses problems. Although Italian spelling is basically phonetic, and does not present the extravagant irregulari-

---

[4]"Un nuovo autografo della *Pellegrina* di G. Bargagli," *La Bibliofilia*, LXXVI (1974), 223-39.

ties of Elizabethan orthography, there are local peculiarities, particularly in texts printed early in the sixteenth century before the reforms of Pietro Bembo: single instead of double consonants, for instance, the Tuscan "ch" instead of "c" before "a" and "o," and those humanist tributes to Greek and Latin, initial "h" and the use of "x" and "y". The editor will then have to decide whether he wants to reproduce the text exactly, whether he wishes to retain some old forms and correct others, or whether he will modernize the text completely. As far as I know, there is no diplomatic text of an Italian Renaissance play, and it is unlikely that one will be prepared. The only satisfactory way of presenting a play of this period in its original form is by facsimile reproduction. This has been contemplated by the Folger Shakespeare Library for some of the Italian plays in its magnificent collection, but has had to be postponed for financial considerations. No other method would be anything but disappointing. There is such a variety of typography, ranging from the almost gothic heavy forms of that first pirated edition of *La Cassaria* to the elegant small italic type which became almost a convention for printing plays later in the century, that a transcription in a modern typeface, no matter how painstaking, would be misleading. Trissino's *Sofonisba* is an extreme example, in a category by itself. The two editions of 1524, in the calligraphic type of Lodovico degli Arrighi, rich in phonetic symbols, have few variants. But the edition of 1529 is in type designed by another calligrapher, Tolomeo Ianiculo, and in it the phonetic symbols for open and close "e" and "o," one of Trissino's innovations, have been reversed. The complications that a diplomatic transcription of this play would involve are too painful to contemplate.

The problems of punctuation I have already mentioned. The more popular a play was and the more frequently it was reprinted, the more it suffered from the cumulative vagaries of editors and printers. Where the manuscript was supplied to the printer by the author, the punctuation of the first edition should be given some consideration, but the punctuation of a pirated or late text deserves no reverence.

Capitalization is also a problem. Renaissance publishers used capitals more liberally than modern publishers, whose house-style generally insists on a democratic uniformity of lower case and lops the heads off all tall poppies. But surely it was a wise provision of philology that in Italian as in Latin all abstractions are feminine. Virtue with a capital and virtue with a small "v" are fish from quite different kettles; liberty with a small "l" may be little more than license or freedom from bonds, but Liberty with a capital is a goddess for whom men are willing to die. It is indeed a pity to annihilate all those transcendental females, inspiring or ominous, dear to the poet as to the artist, who, as Gombrich points out, are both decorative and significant.[5] Even with adjectives, when Trissino writes Regal and Imperial with capitals he reminds his reader of the sacred authority of certain political concepts. Here too the editor should be guided by empathy with the play and its period, and there is surely no reason why a page of a Renaissance tragedy should be indistinguishable from a page of *archy and mehitabel*. Besides, as there are no stage directions in these plays, both punctuation and capitalization are important because they offer some guidance to the actor concerning the style expected of him.

A completely modernized edition would be misleading in many ways, and so far as I know this course has not

---

[5]E.H. Gombrich, "Personification," in *Classical Influences on European Culture A.D. 500-1500,* ed. R.R. Bolgar (Cambridge, 1971), pp. 247-57.

been chosen by any serious editor. The usual practice, common to the Scrittori d'Italia series as well as to Petrocchi and Cerreta, is a discreet modernization, which does not destroy what an eighteenth-century editor calls the patina of the Renaissance period. This eliminates humanist archaisms, expands the contractions which survive from manuscript conventions, such as the barred "p" and the tilde, and yet preserves such northern idiosyncrasies as the use of single instead of double "z" in words like *bellezze*, a characteristic shared by Ariosto and Trissino. Ariosto's use of *nui* and *dui* for *noi* and *due* is also preserved. Punctuation is tactfully modernized in accordance with meaning. The resultant text, then, retains its Renaissance flavour, but presents few difficulties that cannot be explained in the foreword or in notes.

Florindo Cerreta's edition of *L'Alessandro* might well be taken as a model of editorial methods. The introduction gives a detailed account of the history of the play and its fortunes. There is a description of the one manuscript and the twelve printed editions between 1545 and 1611, with a table of the filiations among those versions. Linguistic peculiarities are discussed, morphology, punctuation, and the use of capitals. Historical, literary, and philological notes are added, as well as a glossary and a bibliography.

That edition is a compendium of the problems that confront the editor of a Renaissance comedy once the text of the play has been established. Chief among them, obviously, is language. England, France, and Spain were monarchies, each with a national capital which was also the theatrical and publishing centre. Italy was an association—dissociation might be a better word—of small states exemplifying almost every type of government. There were monarchies, duchies, principalities, republics, papal fiefs, imperial fiefs, each with its own laws, its own coinage and fiscal systems, its own jealously preserved local cus-

toms, and its own dialect. The literary language, universally accepted but to some extent artificial, was Tuscan.
It varied slightly in orthography, as we have seen, according to local pronunciation. With it the writers of comedy
mingled the widest possible vocabulary drawn from the
trades, the professions, and the countryside. Ariosto, for
example, records thieves' slang. Foreigners and dialect-
speaking characters are early introduced: Germans,
Spaniards, and Neapolitans, and the pedant and the lawyer
with their respective macaronic jargons. A writer like
Pietro Aretino, who was Tuscan by birth but spent years
in Rome and Venice, frequenting all levels of society,
commands an extraordinarily rich linguistic amalgam,
which his editor, Giorgio Petrocchi, delights in analyzing.
In all the comedies the young lovers and their merchant
fathers speak a more or less elegant variety of Tuscan,
though it may occasionally show regional solecisms, but
the other characters speak in the idiom of their class or
their region. Consequently the comedies are the most
valuable record we have of the spoken language of the
Renaissance.

The language of the tragedies will demand a different
treatment. Tasso disliked Trissino's simplicity (which is
less simple than it appears at first sight), and he and other
tragic poets used an enriched vocabulary and an increasingly ornate style as the Renaissance moved towards the
baroque, the trend culminating perhaps in Antonio Decio
da Orte's *Acripanda* (1592). The annotator will need to
notice these developments, as well as the individual use of
imagery. The influence of the increasingly popular emblem
books might also be considered.

The study of sources is a serious problem, demanding
as it does a wide range of reading in various literatures.
The authors both of tragedy and of comedy draw more
freely on Italian writers, as well as on a greater variety of

classical authors, than has perhaps been realized. Ariosto unexpectedly quotes Horace in an image that sounds only like a touch of local colour. Trissino echoes Plutarch and Herodotus, as well as Livy, Euripides, and Sophocles, and borrows from both Dante and Petrarch. Ariosto uses stylistic devices as well as plot elements from Boccaccio, and satirizes Petrarchism. Ariosto himself becomes a favourite source as the century progresses, both in his comedies and, with much greater importance for tragedy and tragi-comedy, in his *Orlando Furioso. Acripanda* draws not only on the classics but also on Trissino, Ariosto, Tasso (both *Aminta* and the *Gerusalemme*), and the Old Testament.

The annotator must know intimately the life of the individual cities where the plays were written and, in the case of comedies, set: their ordinances, the character of their people, and their traditions, as well as their contemporary history, so unstable in shifting alliances, so tormented by invasions, sieges, and famines, at intervals too so prosperous, and always so highly civilized.

The annotator of tragedies faces many problems hitherto unsuspected by scholars. Almost no full critical editions of tragedies and pastorals exist, and Cerreta's *Pellegrina* is the unique critical edition, as far as I am aware, of a serious or sentimental comedy. Italian Renaissance tragedy has been so summarily dismissed until recently as spiritless slavish imitation that a wide field is open to an enterprising editor. Typical of this disdain is Petrocchi's cursory treatment of Aretino's *Orazia*, compared to his full commentaries on that author's comedies. Yet Lienhard Bergel, a pioneer in re-evaluation, showed in a brilliant essay in *Renaissance Drama* in 1970 that this play, Augustinian in inspiration, is of great historical importance, and that its heroine, Celia, is an original, articulate creation.[6] In other

---

[6]"The Horatians and Curiatians in the Dramatic and Political-Moralist Literature before Corneille," *Renaissance Drama,* n.s. III (1970), 215-38.

studies too, Bergel has shown the underestimated importance of tragedy in the sixteenth century. There is no
critical edition of *Sofonisba*, or, at the other end of the
century, of Della Valle's *Regina di Scozia*. Ten years ago,
at the first of these conferences, Sam Schoenbaum and
Clifford Leech differed amiably about whether an editor
should use his introduction to present novel and controversial theories. The preface to a critical edition may not
be a suitable place to unveil to the world a new method of
critical approach, para-hermeneutics, for instance, or
geometricalism, but it is surely fitting to set forth there a
fresh, perceptive appraisal of an undervalued or misunder-
stood work.

As for pastoral, the text of the *Pastor fido* presents few
problems, as the 1608 edition was supervised by the
author. But Luigi Fasso's reprint in the Classici italiani
series (1950) gives a minimum of annotation. Guidobaldo
Bonarelli's almost equally popular and influential *Filli di
Sciro* came out in the Scrittori d'Italia series in 1941. The
1941 text is based on the 1607 edition and, as is cus-
tomary with that series, has only bibliographical notes.
There is no true critical edition of Tasso's *Aminta*. The
numerous romantic comedies of the late sixteenth century
in which at last the heroine plays an important role, and
which are so rich in sentiment, must still be read in their
original editions.

As I hope this paper has made plain, a wide field lies
open invitingly to the aspiring editor of Italian plays.

EDITING SPANISH *COMEDIAS*
OF THE XVIITH CENTURY:
HISTORY AND PRESENT-DAY PRACTICE

Arnold G. Reichenberger

PRELIMINARY REMARKS

Ladies and Gentlemen. Please allow me to recall to your mind some basic data about the theatre of the Spanish Golden Age. The Golden Age or *Siglo de Oro* in general extends from the 1480s into the second half of the seventeenth century. The development of the theatre begins in the 1490s with Juan del Encina and ends in 1681 with the death of Calderón de la Barca.

This span of two hundred years is clearly divided into two periods of roughly one hundred years each: the theatre before Lope de Vega, *el teatro prelopista*, from Juan del Encina to the appearance of Lope de Vega, and the theatre of and after Lope de Vega, the theatre of the *comedia*. Lope dominated the Spanish theatre of the seventeenth century; and his achievement, the Spanish theatre as we understand it by the term *comedia*, lived on even beyond the death of Calderón, the last creative dramatic poet of Spain. The one hundred years after Lope are again divided into two periods of about equal length, although the break is far from being as sharp as the one between the *teatro prelopista* and the *comedia*. The second of these periods begins with the appearance of Calderón around 1630. His most famous play *La vida es sueño* ("Life is a Dream") is dated about 1635, the year of Lope's death.

Now, a word about the term *comedia*. The plays are called *comedias* because, while not free of violent emotions, death, and elements of tragedy, they end with order restored. *Comedia* is usually and correctly rendered "drama" or "play." What Lope's genius achieved was far-reaching: he created what can be called a formula for the Spanish theatre. Within this formula, a play consists of three acts, averaging 1,000 verses each, and is composed in a variety of verse forms. The structure is free-wheeling, sometimes episodic. It seems that Lope, dramatic poet that he was, is often so completely carried away by the scene he is developing that he does not pay attention to its structural importance or non-importance; thus he may be called Lope de Vega, *poeta del momento*. There is a strong lyrical strain in him. As a matter of fact, he is one of the triad of Spanish poets of the seventeenth century, together with Góngora and Quevedo. Other playwrights have their own characteristics and with Calderón the *comedia* becomes, let us say, more stabilized, the thought content more philosophical along the lines of post-Tridentine philosophy and theology. Calderón is the recognized master of *autos sacramentales*, the religious plays performed in public (not in the theatres) each year on Corpus Christi day. Their characters are allegorical figures.

Now we come to the subject of this paper: editing Spanish *comedias* of the seventeenth century: history and present-day practice.

I. The Communication of the Texts to the Reading Public, 1600-1800.

A. The Printed Texts.

If we take the term "editing" in the modern sense, to mean editing with some degree at least of textual criticism, we can expect little "editing" in this period; editing is in general virtually synonymous with publishing. And a play can appear in print: (1) as part of a collection of plays by a single author; (2) as part of a collection of plays by various authors; (3) as a single independent publication, unbound, for which we use the Spanish term *suelta* (literally "loose," "not connected"), meaning *edición suelta* ("separate edition").

Our main and absolutely indispensable source of bibliographical and biographical information about the *comedia* and its playwrights is Cayetano Alberto de la Barrera y Leirado, *Catálogo bibliográfico y biográfico del teatro antiguo español desde sus orígenes hasta mediados del siglo XVIII* (Madrid, 1860). This catalogue has been reproduced twice in recent years (London, 1968, and Madrid, 1969). Since 1860, of course, many bibliographical studies for individual authors have appeared, above all for Lope de Vega, but as a comprehensive bibliography for the Spanish theatre of the Golden Age La Barrera's work has not been superseded.

(1) Collections of Plays by a Single Author.

(a) Lope Félix de Vega Carpio (1562-1635)

There is a relatively limited number of such collections in proportion to the number of playwrights, yet one collection is outstanding for the number of volumes it comprises: the twenty-five volumes, called *partes,* of the *Comedias de Lope de Vega.* They extend in time and place from Volume I, Valencia, 1604, to Volume XXV, Zaragoza, 1647. La Barrera (p. 424) counts 290 *comedias* in Lope's collected plays, 76 in the collections of various authors, and 37 in *suelta* editions, a total of 403 plays, plus a number of plays attributed to Lope but of doubtful authenticity. Lope himself, in two lists of 1603 and 1618 respectively, names 427 titles of which 253 have survived in manuscript or in print.[1] Morley and Bruerton, *Chronology*, recognize 135 *comedias* as authentic Lope plays and 186 of doubtful authenticity. [2]

All *partes* but two, XXI and XXIII, appeared in more than one edition, at various times and in various places. All of these were known to bibliographers at some time or other, but many are no longer extant, and some also may be ghost editions. *Parte* I had the greatest number of editions. It appeared altogether fifteen times between 1604 and 1626: in Valencia (three times), Valladolid (three), Madrid (two), Zaragoza (three), Lisbon (one), Amberes (Antwerp) (one), Brussels (one), Milan (one). It is easy to see that so many editions constitute many problems for the textual critic.

(b) Pedro Calderón de la Barca (1600-1681)

Calderón's production compared with Lope's prolific output was relatively modest. He wrote "only" 120 *comedias* and 96 *autos sacramentales*. The basic edition of his *comedias* is by Juan de Vera Tassis y Villaroel (who calls himself *"su mayor amigo"*), and consists of nine volumes. The nine volumes appeared in Madrid, 1682-91, by Francisco Sanz, *"impresor del Reino"* ("printer of the realm").

Vera Tassis had predecessors, the foremost being Pedro Calderón's brother José, who issued a *Primera parte* in Madrid in 1640, *"recogidos y sacados de sus verdaderos originales"* ("collected and taken from the genuine originals"), followed by the *Segunda parte* (Madrid, 1641).

---

[1]Hugo A. Rennert, *Bibliography of the Dramatic Works of Lope de Vega Carpio. Based upon the Catalogue of John Rutter Chorley* (Extrait de la *Revue Hispanique*, XXXIII; New York and Paris, 1915), p. 130.

[2]S. Griswold Morley and Courtney Bruerton, *The Chronology of Lope de Vega's "Comedias"* (New York, 1940). There is a Spanish edition, revised by Morley (Madrid, 1968).

Partes III, IV, V were published by others: III in 1664; IV in 1674 with a Prologue by Calderón himself; V–repudiated by Calderón–in 1677 in Barcelona (actually Madrid). The Vera Tassis collection, in turn, was reproduced by Juan Fernández de Apontes (Madrid, 1760-65), *"invirtiendo completamente el orden de las piezas"* ("completely reversing the sequence of the plays").[3]

There exist several one-volume editions of Calderón's *autos sacramentales*, printed before the first collection appeared, published by Pedro de Pando y Mier, in six volumes, and printed by Manuel Ruiz de Murga (Madrid, 1717). The next edition is that by Juan Fernández de Apontes (Madrid, 1759-60). It is nothing but a reprint of the Pando y Mier edition, with the sequence of the volumes completely changed.[4]

(c) Collections of Other Single Authors

There is no time and probably it is not necessary to enumerate the other authors who have collections of their own. I will only mention the enigmatic *Segunda parte de las comedias del maestro Tirso de Molina, recogida por su sobrino don Francisco Lucas de Avila* ("collected by his nephew") (Madrid, 1635). It contains Tirso's most famous play, *El burlador de Sevilla*, the Don Juan play, but also many plays of doubtful authenticity. Tirso himself says in the Prologue that four plays in this volume are not his, but he does not say which.[5]

[3]La Barrera, p. 336.

[4]La Barrera, p. 58

[5]Edward M. Wilson and Duncan Moir, *The Golden Age: Drama 1492-1700* (London and New York, 1971), p. 91; part of *A Literary History of Spain*, ed. R.O. Jones, consisting of 8 volumes, not consecutively numbered.

(2) Collections of Plays by Various Authors.

José Simón Díaz, *Manual,* lists a total of thirty-nine of these collections published between 1609 and 1796.[6] Most of them are one-volume publications. They include not only *comedias* and *autos sacramentales* but also shorter farcical plays called *entremeses* ("interludes") and similar pieces.

However, there is one outstanding collection. Its title is *Comedias nuevas escogidas de los mejores ingenios de España* ("New plays selected from the best creative minds of Spain") and consists of forty-eight *partes* published between 1652 and 1704. It is usually cited in the abbreviated form *Comedias nuevas escogidas* or simply the *Escogidas Collection.* There is a considerable lapse of time between *Parte* XLVII (1681) and *Parte* XLVIII (1704). Volumes I-XLVII were published almost regularly, one each year, although there are gaps of several years between some volumes. However, more than one consecutive volume was published in some years, as many as four (XVI-XIX) in 1662. There is another earlier collection, known as *Comedias de diferentes autores* (1611-1652), which is bibliographically very complex.[7]

You may ask how bibliographical unity or consistency was established over the decades. The significant part of the title page of *Parte* I reads: *"Primera parte de comedias escogidas de los mejores ingenios de España...* Madrid, por Domingo García y Morrás a costa de Juan de San Vicente, mercader de libros, 1652." This means that the bookseller Juan de San Vicente gave the order to print to the printshop of Domingo García y Morrás. The volumes are consecutively numbered with the title formula as intro-

---

[6] José Simón Díaz, *Manual de Bibliografía de la literatura española,* 2nd edn. (Barcelona, 1966), pp. 115-16.

[7] See La Barrera, pp. 683-7.

duced for *Parte* I appearing with some variations on the title page of almost all the volumes. However, publisher and printer change, but not the place of publication, which is always Madrid. The appearance of the volumes of the *Escogidas Collection* and the willingness of the publishers to invest can only mean that there had developed a substantial reading public for the plays of the *comedia*.

(3) *Suelta* Editions.

The trend of the reading public interested in the *comedia* continued through the eighteenth century. The demand was now primarily satisfied by *suelta* editions, which dominated the market. These editions are paperbound and consist on the average of sixteen folios, with or without a colophon indicating publisher, place, and year of publication.

From the outset one would assume that these editions, reprints of other texts closer to the original, are not of major value for the establishment of a reliable text. But no one knows for sure. At any rate every textual critic has to find out whether *suelta* editions exist and he has to evaluate them as to their importance for the history of the text on which he is working.

Twelve *suelta* editions sometimes were bound together and published with a title page, as another edition of an already existing *parte* in the collection of a single author or of a collection of various authors. These editions are easily distinguished from the genuine volume because they have no continuous foliation. Furthermore, private bibliophiles interested in the *comedia* assembled *sueltas* in bound volumes. In the University of Pennsylvania Rare Book Collection there are twenty-four such volumes collected by the Imperial Ambassador Count Bonaventura Harrach during his three assignments to the court in Madrid in 1664, 1673-76, and 1697-98.

B. Manuscripts.

In principle, a manuscript text has neither more nor less authority than a printed text. There is, however, one obvious exception to this rule: the autograph or, strictly speaking, the holograph manuscript, written in its entirety by the playwright himself and signed by him. We are particularly fortunate in the case of Lope de Vega. Forty-three autograph manuscripts have survived, not all of them published in scholarly editions.[8] Also in respect to Lope de Vega, another exception has to be made. I am speaking of the so-called Gálvez manuscripts. Ignacio de Gálvez was an (or the) archivist in 1762 for the house of the Duke of Sessa, a descendant of the Duke of Sessa whose private secretary Lope de Vega was. The Duke was Lope's patron and the first collector of autograph manuscripts of his *comedias*. Gálvez copied thirty-two Lope plays with the date of composition in Lope's hand and his signature at the end. Gálvez is, on the whole, considered to have been a faithful copyist so that the Gálvez copies are of crucial importance for the chronology of Lope's plays and for establishing an authentic text. We will have to come back to the Gálvez manuscripts shortly.[9]

Just a brief word about Calderonian manuscripts. There are 418 dramatic manuscripts catalogued in Simón Díaz's *Bibliografía*.[10] Twenty-four of these are autographs, most of them autograph in their entirety, some of them only

---

[8]See Walter Poesse, *The Internal Line-Structure of Thirty Autograph Plays of Lope de Vega* (Bloomington, 1949); a list of forty-two autographs is on pp. 83-8, to which add *El primero Benavides* (1600).

[9]See Augustín G. de Amezúa, *Una colección manuscrita y desconocida de comedias de Lope de Vega Carpio* (Centro de Estudios sobre Lope de Vega, cuaderno núm. 1; Madrid, 1945).

[10]José Simón Díaz, *Bibliografía de las literaturas hispánicas*, VII (Madrid, 1967), pp. 63-96.

partially. Some are signed by Calderón. A few scholarly editions of Calderonian autograph manuscript *comedias* have recently appeared. Most of the autographs are kept in Madrid libraries. However, there must be more manuscripts of Calderón's *comedias* and *autos sacramentales* in existence. The Hispanic Society of America in New York has thirty-eight manuscripts, most of them *autos*. Three of originally five manuscripts were found in 1959 by Professor Václav Cerný in the library of Kuenburg Castle in Mladá Vožice in Czechoslovakia. One of these was a hitherto unknown play, *El gran Duque de Gandía*, published by Professor Cerný in 1963.

An autograph may be a fair copy or it may show corrections by the playwright himself and/or by others such as the theatrical producer. The playwright may have given the draft to a theatrical company or possibly in some cases to the bookseller. Furthermore, the autograph may not even be the most authentic last version of the play. The poet may have later modified his work to a greater or lesser degree, and the modifications could then appear in the printed text. Another note of caution concerning so-called autographs: proud nineteenth-century collectors were only too ready to declare their cherished possession an autograph. Actually, the determination of a manuscript as an autograph is possible only if it is signed by the author or if a sufficient number of genuine autographs are available with which to compare the manuscript in question.

C. Evaluation of the Textual Transmission, 1600-1800.

We have come to the end of our necessarily brief and selective bibliographical sketch. Now we shall consider the value of these publications in their reliability concerning the text and the problem of authorship.

Excluding for the moment those manuscripts which can be definitely established as genuine autographs, we must state that the texts have to be approached with the greatest caution, both as to their accuracy and as to authorship. Modern scholarship has made considerable contributions toward clarifying these problems, as we shall see later. But for the moment we shall consider the important preliminary question of how the plays reached the printer in the first place, and of the source of the manuscripts.

I am not aware of any comprehensive study of these problems. However, some piecemeal information is available. We know that Lope de Vega wrote his plays for the directors of theatrical companies, called *autores*, or for specific actors and actresses. We know, furthermore, that plays were traded among the directors of these companies. And the extant dramatic manuscripts often show visible traces of preparation of the plays for performance, with portions marked by *sí* or *no* in the margin of the page to indicate whether the passage so marked should be performed or omitted. But that still does not explain how the written texts got into print. In the case of some plays, we know that the theatres were what we would today call "bugged." There were a few people known as *grandes memorias* who sat through several performances and wrote down what they remembered. They were, of course, hired by the booksellers. These cases, however, must have been exceptional. Normally, more than one manuscript copy of any play must have existed within a company, for memorizing roles, for prompting, and for similar purposes, all copies ultimately deriving from the original, with or without textual changes wrought by the stage director. These copies must then have been sold to the bookseller. It is easy to see the number of errors which might occur during the manuscript's journey from the playwright through the performing companies to the printer.

As for the problem of authenticity of authorship, we have the complaints of the playwrights themselves. I have already mentioned Tirso de Molina's remarks in the Prologue of his *Segunda parte*. Lope de Vega claimed to have edited his plays himself from *Parte* IX to *Parte* XX because he was disgusted with the distortions his own texts had previously suffered. Lope's outbursts are numerous throughout his life.[11] One example must suffice. In the Prologue to *Parte* XVII (1621) Lope invents two lawsuits by the allegorical character *El Teatro* against the book-sellers. The booksellers win each time because they prove that once the playwrights (*"los ingenios"*) are paid they no longer have any rights at all to their plays (*"no tenían acción sobre ellas"*). There exists complete chaos: the *autores* steal the plays from each other or they sell them to the towns which need them for their festivities. They insert other verses where it pleases them, or they steal or buy these from playwrights' secretaries (*"papelistas y secretarios cómicos"*). Lope ends by complaining that the most harmful thing for an author is to have his *comedias* printed. The poet cannot control the publication — especially when he never even kept a copy of his work.[12]

Calderón in *Parte* IV (Madrid, 1674) complains about the changes (*"yerros"*) in his own plays but also about the publishing of others' plays under Calderón's name, and the cutting off of the end of an act or even of a play just to save paper.[13] Copyright protection was weak. The *privilegios* were granted only for ten years and were limited to a province. Therefore the booksellers could easily capitalize on famous names.

[11]See Lope Félix de Vega Carpio, *La Dorotea*, ed. Edwin S. Morby (2nd edn., revised; Berkeley and Los Angeles, 1968), p. 54, n. 18.

[12]See Américo Castro and Hugo A. Rennert, *Vida de Lope de Vega (1562-1635)* (Salamanca, etc., 1968), p. 262.

[13]Simón Díaz, *Bibliografía*, VII, p. 59.

The booksellers claimed authenticity for their texts sometimes by calling their *partes* *"perfecta"* or *"verdadera."* On what basis they made these claims is not known. In some cases they advertised in their title pages *"sacadas de los originales"* ("taken from the originals"). But of what nature were the originals? The playwright's autograph manuscript or a copy directly derived from it? Probably not.

I realize that the information provided here is very spotty. What is needed at this time is a systematic collection of the facts so far known and a further search through title pages and the preliminary material of seventeenth-century collections.

There is, however, a deeper reason for authorship confusion. The *comedia* is the most powerful national theatre in existence, in that it expresses in dramatic-poetic form the ideals of the Spanish people of its time (i.e., of the first decades of the seventeenth century). And it was the genius of Lope de Vega—the genius of conformity—which had created the *comedia*'s structural formula, its thematology, and particularly its poetic language with its metaphors and imagery. Since "literature," that is, poetry, was in the air, Lope could be imitated, or, more accurately, Lope's formula could be used as a vehicle of expression by any fairly gifted writer. Thus it was really Lope himself who, in the last analysis, is the cause of the confusion. No wonder, then, that the problem of authorship plagues present-day scholarship. But may I add the somewhat heretical opinion that it is not so terribly important to attribute plays to specific authors. The *comedia* is a collective enterprise, which can be compared to Spanish balladry, the *Romancero*, the texts of which underwent many transformations in their transmission through space and time.[14]

[14]Castro and Rennert, pp. 262-3.

II. Scholarship and Editorial Practices, 1800-1975.

The Romantic Period, as you all know, brought about a deep interest in the history and literature of nations, and not only of scholars' own nations but also of whole regions, as part of an all-embracing history of the humanities. The first histories of Spanish literature appeared in Germany (1804), in France (1813), and in North America and in England (1849). Friedrich Bouterweck in 1804 dedicated Volume III of his *Geschichte der neueren Poesie und Beredsamkeit* to Spain. It formed in itself part of his *Geschichte der Künste und Wissenschaften*. J. Ch. L. Simonde de Sismondi in 1813 wrote *De la littérature du midi de l'Europe*, of which Volumes III and IV deal with *Histoire de la littérature espagnole*. Finally, we have George Ticknor's *History of Spanish Literature* (New York and London, 1849) in three volumes. All three works were translated in due time into Spanish. The first history of Spanish literature written by a Spaniard is Antonio Gil de Zárate's *Resumen histórico de la literature española* (Madrid, 1844).

The most urgent need, in satisfying the re-awakened interest in the study of literature, was to make the texts widely accessible. We shall restrict ourself to the theatre and proceed as far as possible in chronological order. The first attempt to create a collection of the Spanish theatre was made before the beginning of the nineteenth century. Vicente García de la Huerta, a successful dramatist in his own right, published *Theatro Hespañol* in sixteen volumes (Madrid, 1785-86). Despite the general title, the collection is limited to plays by Calderón and his contemporaries and to the editor's own plays. Much more ambitious was Eugenio de Ochoa. He edited *Colección de los mejores autores españoles* in sixty volumes (Paris, 1838-72). The first six volumes bear the title *Tesoro del teatro español desde su origen (año de 1356) hasta nuestros días; arreg-*

lado y dividido en cuatro partes por Eugenio de Ochoa
("Treasures of the Spanish Theatre from its origin (in the
year 1356) until the present; arranged and divided into
four parts by Eugenio de Ochoa") (Paris, 1838-40). For
the first time the Spanish theatre is presented in chronological sequence: Vol. I, Theatre before Lope de Vega; II,
Lope de Vega; III, Calderón; IV, Major Dramatists, contemporaries of Lope and Calderón; V, Other Dramatists
of the second half of the seventeenth and eighteenth and
early nineteenth centuries. Vol. VI (1840) is an anthology
from the preceding five volumes. The scholarly intent of
Ochoa's *Tesoro* is obvious from its organization.

From German romanticism and its preference for
Calderón came the edition of his *comedias* by Juan Jorge
Keil, in four volumes (Leipzig, 1827-30). In the title the
editor claims that the texts were "*cotejadas* ["collated"]
*con las mejores ediciones hasta ahora publicadas, corregi-
das y dadas a luz por . . . .*" The sequence of 108 plays
follows exactly the Vera Tassis edition. At the beginning
of Volume IV we find plaintive observations about the
unreliability of the texts due to the sloppiness and looseness of editorial policy of the printers and publishers. For
a final fifth volume Keil promises to list variants in the
most important editions, to offer notes explaining difficult
passages and proper names, to indicate the sources of the
plots, and to speculate about the time of composition of
the plays. Volume V unfortunately never appeared. We
have to wait until 1890 when a comparable enterprise was
undertaken by the Royal Spanish Academy in publishing
the plays by Lope (see below).

The year 1846 is a milestone in the history of Spanish
literature. In that year the enterprising printer Manuel
Rivadeneyra (1805-72) published in Madrid the first
volume of the fundamental collection *Biblioteca de
Autores Españoles* (*BAE*), which made easily accessible

the texts of Spanish literature up to the early nineteenth century. By 1880, seventy-one volumes had appeared, including the Index. The *BAE* is now (from 1954) being reprinted and much enlarged; the last volume (CCLXVIII) on the shelves of the University of Pennsylvania Library is dated 1974. The *Comedia*, including the *autos sacramentales*, is represented in altogether sixteen volumes: Lope in four, Calderón in four, *Dramáticos contemporáneos a Lope de Vega* in two, etc. The editors Juan Eugenio Hartzenbusch (for Lope, Calderón, and Tirso de Molina) and Ramón de Mesonero Romanos (for *Dramáticos contemporáneos*) were writers and critics rather than scholars. Hartzenbusch, like García de la Huerta before him, was a dramatist. Hartzenbusch was well aware of the wretched condition of his copy texts, and tried to correct some of the more obvious mistakes. Some other passages he "improved" as he saw fit. In addition, he divided the acts into scenes. But more accurate editions will appear in the future, he declares. The merit of having made available so many plays to the public far outweighs the unreliability of the texts, unavoidable at that time. Unfortunately, the faulty texts of the *BAE* volumes are still carried on in many modern uncritical commercial publications of *comedias*.

We encounter a scholarly edition of a collection for the first time in 1887. I am referring to the two volumes of *Ocho comedias desconocidas*, edited by Adolf Schaeffer.[15] Schaeffer is the author of the *Geschichte des spanischen Nationaldramas* (Leipzig, 1890), a work actually limited to the theatre of the Golden Age. The eight plays are reprinted from a volume of twelve, evidently a *parte*, the

[15] *Ocho comedias desconocidas de don Guillem de Castro, del Licenciado Damian Salustio del Poyo, de Luis Vélez de Guevara etc. tomadas de un libro antiguo de comedias, nuevamente hallado y dadas a luz por Adolf Schaeffer* (Leipzig, 1887), 2 vols.

title and the usual preliminaries wanting, and consisting of 309 numbered leaves. Schaeffer successfully tries to determine the date of the volume, between 1612 and 1618, from the evidence available. As to the establishment of a reliable text, he complains about the impossibility *"de fijar un texto puro y exacto al mismo tiempo"* ("to establish a text which would be both pure and exact"), about misprints, and about looseness of plot structure and the syntax of the dramatists. He makes very few attempts at emendation and has practically no notes. His scholarship, then, is limited to determining the date of the volume. In addition, he briefly discusses each of the twelve plays, mostly from the bibliographical point of view.

We now proceed to consider the modern editions of Lope de Vega and of Calderón. But we have first to say a few words about the founder of modern scholarship and criticism of Spanish literature, Marcelino Menéndez Pelayo (1856-1912). His knowledge of the ancient classics and of Spanish literature of the late Middle Ages and the two centuries of the Golden Age was encyclopedic. It can truly be said that his achievements gave the initial impulse to the literary-historical studies in this area which are being carried on in Spain and abroad at the present time. The first part of his life was dedicated to the history of theology and of aesthetics, but later the direction of his investigations veered toward literary history. He published an *Antología de poetas líricos castellanos* (1890-1908) and *Orígenes de la novela* (1905-10). They contain both texts and very extensive historical and evaluative studies. And here is where the *comedia* comes in. In 1890 he began to edit the *Obras de Lope de Vega*, consisting of fifteen volumes by 1913, under the auspices of the Real Academia Española. This was a "monumental" edition in the literal sense of the word. The volumes are printed on heavy paper, and the texts are amply spaced, so that the

Academy Edition looks more like a monument to the memory of Lope de Vega than a book that physically can be handled with ease. Menéndez Pelayo's introductions are still invaluable, primarily for his investigations into the sources of the plays at hand, supported by extensive excerpts from them. These sources include chronicles, Italian *novelle, romances* ("ballads") and so forth. Menéndez Pelayo's aesthetic judgment, his evaluation of the plays, is to be understood in the light of the prevailing standards of his time and of his personal preferences and prejudices. He was a classicist and an orthodox Catholic, but he was also an ardent Spaniard. I think that his deeprooted integration (like Lope's own) into what globally is termed *españolismo* ("Spanishness") is the reason for his finely tuned sensibility to the values of Lope's theatre, although this theatre is or at least seems to be running counter to the orderly structure of the classical play of antiquity.

Menéndez Pelayo expounded sound editorial principles in the *Observaciones generales* to his edition of Lope's plays. However, considering the magnitude of the project and the purpose of the Academy edition, he settles for the middle road between an edition destined for the general public ("*edición vulgar*") and a critical edition.[16] A collation of the autograph manuscripts of *Carlos V en Francia* and *El primero Benavides* shows that in most cases the Academy edition follows the *parte* text; in these two instances, however, the autograph manuscripts were not available to Menéndez Pelayo.

After Menéndez Pelayo's death, the edition of Lope's plays was continued from 1916 to 1930, in the *Nueva edición de la Real Academia Española de las obras de*

---

[16]See Menéndez Pelayo, *Estudios sobre el teatro de Lope de Vega*, I (Santander, 1949), pp. 11-20. (Edición Nacional de las obras completas de Menéndez Pelayo, XXIX.)

Lope de Vega under the general editorship of Emilio Cotarelo y Mori, with the plays edited by himself and others.

Nothing at all was done for Calderón at this time. Menéndez Pelayo, in his formative years, was not particularly attracted to him, and was even repulsed by Calderón's bloody honor plays, although he later changed his opinion. So his contribution to Calderón studies is limited to the collection of his lectures under the title *Calderón y su teatro. Conferencias,* published at the occasion of the bicentenary of Calderón's death in 1881.

Finally we come to the first critical edition of a *comedia.* The French Hispanist Alfred Morel-Fatio in 1877 edited the autograph manuscript of Calderón's *El mágico prodigioso* ("The Miracle-Working Magician"). This manuscript is the first draft of the play, but it is incomplete in the sense that Calderón did not write the conclusion, though the manuscript is of the quite unusual length of 3722 lines. In the Introduction Morel-Fatio discusses the sources of the play, offers a critical analysis, speaks about scene division in the *comedia,* and has observations about language and versification in *El mágico.* At the end he describes the manuscript and gives the bibliography of the subsequent printed editions and translations. The text is supported by a critical apparatus, consisting of the manuscript reading and its corrections put in by Calderón himself, and the collation with the *princeps* of 1663 and with *Parte* VI of the Vera Tassis edition of 1683 and the nineteenth-century editions by Keil and Hartzenbusch. The topics touched on in the Introduction and the variants noted at the foot of the page set a pattern which is still more or less followed today.

The next decade sees the remarkable editions by Max Krenkel of four Calderonian plays: *La vida es sueño* and *El príncipe constante* (1881); *El mágico prodigioso*

(1885); *El alcalde* ["mayor"] *de Zalamea* (1887). His models were the German annotated editions of the ancient classics. All four editions have source studies which become more extensive, with ample excerpts, from edition to edition. The texts of *La vida* and *El príncipe* are based on Hartzenbusch, collated with Keil. For the text of *El mágico* Morel-Fatio's edition was a firm basis. The distinction of the *Alcalde* edition is that Krenkel was able to give not only Calderón's text but also that of the play of the same title attributed to Lope, from a rare *suelta*. The Calderonian *Alcalde* text is based on the *princeps*, a *suelta* of 1651, collated with Vera Tassis, *Parte* VII (1683), Keil, and Hartzenbusch. Krenkel is the first editor who supplies ample annotation to the text itself. His main procedure is to illuminate the text in hand with parallel passages from other plays, mostly but not exclusively Calderonian: which reveals his uncommonly wide reading (and an excellently organized card file). Furthermore, there are detailed grammatical and stylistic annotations in the manner found in commentaries on Latin and Greek texts.

Another twenty-five years go by until rigorous philological scholarship takes root in Spain under the leadership of Ramón Menéndez Pidal (1869-1968). He was primarily a medievalist and a linguist, but he also contributed to the study of the *comedia* by initiating the series of critical editions of autographs known as *Teatro Antiguo Español*, sponsored by the *Centro de Estudios Históricos* (founded in 1910). Menéndez Pidal opened the series himself in 1916 with the edition of *La serrana* ["mountain maid"] *de la Vera* by Luis Vélez de Guevara, prepared by him and his wife. Editions of nine plays have appeared, the last in 1940. These editions aim at a text established with the maximum precision the source material permits. The spelling of the autograph manuscript is exactly reproduced, *"pues sin este respeto fundamental no puede haber la*

exactitud necesaria para la crítica del texto" ("because
without this fundamental respect there cannot be the
exactness indispensable to textual criticism").[17] Accentu-
ation and punctuation are modernized. This is still the
present-day practice. In the *Observaciones y notas* the
editors study dramatic works with related themes. The
practice has been followed by later editors, but I do not
know whether in all those scholarly editions where such a
study would have been possible. In the edition of Lope's
El primero Benavides, [18] we followed the example set by
William L. Fichter, editor of Lope's autograph manuscript
of *El sembrar* ["sowing"] *en buena tierra* (New York,
1944).

There is one major achievement which remains to be
mentioned: the successful search for objective criteria to
establish authorship and at least an approximate date for
the composition of a *comedia.* These criteria are two: (1)
the study of the versification of an author; (2) an almost
clinical observation of an author's orthöepy. The first
study concentrating on Lope with emphasis on versification is by Milton A. Buchanan, *The Chronology of Lope
de Vega's Plays* (Toronto, 1922). Buchanan studied Lope's
preferences for nine metres in dated plays from 1593 to
1635 and in twelve plays by three other playwrights. He
established the frequency of use of each metre in each
play in terms of percentages. Thus the first play, *El favor
agradecido* ("A favor gratefully received") of 1593, has
55% *redondillas,* 13% *quintillas,* and 5% *romance,* all
native Spanish metres, and 22% Italianate verses, that is,

[17]See Luis Vélez de Guevara, *La serrana de la Vera,* eds. R. Menéndez Pidal
and M. Goyri de Menéndez Pidal (Teatro Antiguo Español, I; Madrid, 1916),
p. vii.

[18]Lope Félix de Vega Carpio, *El primero Benavides,* eds. Arnold G. Reichenberger and Augusta E. Foley (Philadelphia, 1973).

eleven-syllable lines. In the last play of 1634, *Las bizarrías* ["gallantry"] *de Belisa*, there are only 22% *redondillas*, no *quintillas*, but 54% *romance* and 11% *décimas* (which appear only twice before ca. 1605-11). Buchanan illustrates orthöepy through the example of the word *diablo* which can be either a two-syllable or a three-syllable word. After a number of preliminary studies by S. Griswold Morley, which go back to 1905, of the versification of other playwrights, in 1940 the team of S. Griswold Morley and Courtney Bruerton published their monumental *The Chronology of Lope de Vega's Comedias* (New York). They succeeded in dating, at least within certain limited time spaces, 314 plays, and cautiously stated their opinion about 186 plays of doubtful or not certain authenticity which were printed under Lope's name. Their findings were confirmed through the above-mentioned Gálvez manuscripts. In seventeen cases checked the ratio between right and wrong was 82.35:17.65.[19]

Much of what is to be said about present-day practice is implicit in my survey of editorial techniques in the nineteenth and twentieth centuries. A great number of scholarly editions of single plays have appeared in the last half century, mostly in England, Canada, and the United States. This is not the place to give you a sort of spoken review article of recent editions. Instead, with due immodesty, I shall speak mainly about my own experiences. I have published one edition (Granada, 1956) based on printed texts, Luis Vélez de Guevara's *El embuste acreditado* ("The successful trick"), and two editions (Philadelphia, 1963 and 1973) based on autographs by Lope, *Carlos V en Francia* and *El primero Benavides*, the latter with Augusta E. Foley. I shall speak first about the editorial problems presented by the text, both printed and

[19]Amezúa, p. 22.

autograph. Next, I shall discuss the Introduction and finally the Notes.

Altogether sixteen editions are recorded for the Vélez play, either printed or manuscript, and under various titles and variously attributed to Luis Vélez de Guevara, his son Juan, Rey de Artieda, and Juan de Zabaleta. The text resulting from the collation of the nine available texts is based on the *princeps*, appearing in the *Quinta parte* (Madrid, 1653) of the *Escogidas Collection*, but incorporates the text published in *Parte treinta y cuatro* (Madrid, 1670) of the same collection under the title *El disparate creído* ("Crazy jokes believed") with Juan de Zabaleta as the author, and a manuscript with still another title, *Otro demonio tenemos* ("Another ghost we got"), by *tres ingenios*. Each edition has passages the other editions do not have. I decided to print everything I found: in other words, to create a composite text. Is this the original Vélez text? I doubt it. The corrections and modifications by stage directors or censors, changes by printers, and a possible *refundición* ("adaptation") by Zabaleta are included in the text. We have, in short, a classic example of how a play, under the prevailing circumstances, became public property.

The text is reproduced with spelling, accents, and punctuation modernized except when the ancient orthography reflects actual pronunciation; strophic division is marked by indentation. The verses are numbered and the corresponding pages or folios are indicated in the margins. If a verse is shared by two or, as sometimes in Calderón, by three speakers, each fraction of the verse goes into a new line, not flush with the beginning of the verse but moved one space to the right of where the first part of the verse ends in the preceding line. The variant readings are listed at the foot of the page.

Considering the bibliographical conditions of the

comedia, of which the Vélez text is a typical example, it will not surprise anyone that no critical edition of the total work of any playwright has been attempted. Only in the case of Calderón have preliminary bibliographical studies been undertaken, mainly by H.C. Heaton and his pupil Everett W. Hesse in the 1940s and by Edward M. Wilson and his pupil Don W. Cruickshank since 1959.[20] In 1973 D.W. Cruickshank and J.E. Varey published "reliable [facsimile] reprints of the first editions of all nine *partes de comedias* [by Calderón] and, in the case of the first five *partes*, of the reprints which appeared during his lifetime."[21] In nineteen volumes they "[make] available. . . the material necessary for a textual study of all those works which appeared in the collective volumes of his plays in the course of the seventeenth century."[21] This edition means a most significant new beginning of serious textual criticism, not only for Calderón, but for all dramatists.

Professor Hans Flasche, University of Hamburg, is circulating libraries in Spain to obtain information about their holdings of Calderonian manuscripts. He aims at producing a critical edition of the *autos*, hopefully for 1981, the tercentenary of Calderón's death. In addition, between 1962-63 and 1975 he has published a critical edition of Calderón's *auto sacramental La vida es sueño* (which is the religious version of the play) in five installments which he calls *"Bausteine* ["building blocks"] *zu einer kritischen und kommentierten Ausgabe Calderóns."*[22]

---

[20] See Wilson and Moir, pp. 160-1.

[21] Pedro Calderón de la Barca, *Comedias*, facsimile edition, 19 vols., eds. D.W. Cruickshank and John Varey (London, 1973), I, vii.

[22] Hans Flasche, "Bausteine zu einer kritischen und kommentierten Ausgabe Calderóns," no. 1, "Beitrag zu einer kritischen und kommentierten Ausgabe des Auto sacramental 'La vida es sueño' von Calderón," in *Homenaje a Johannes Vincke*, II (Madrid, 1962-63). The other four *Beiträge* appear in *Gesammelte Aufsätze zur Kulturgeschichte Spaniens*, XXI (1963), XXII (1965), XXV (1970), and XXVIII (1975).

The editorial problems presented by the autograph manuscripts are relatively simple. Assuming that the autograph is the final form of the play, we have the authoritative text before us. Thus the editor's task is to read or sometimes to decipher the manuscript. In the case of the two Lope plays reading and transcribing the text was a relatively easy task, since Lope's handwriting, even when he writes in haste, is quite legible. And the presentation of the text on the printed page is not different from that of the text derived from printed editions, with the fundamental exception, of course, of respecting the spelling of the autograph. However, the exciting part of editing an autograph manuscript I have not mentioned yet: deciphering the corrections in Lope's own hand, that is, trying to read or to make out the deleted words. Lope himself always tried to make the discarded version more or less illegible, either by a series of loops or—less frequently—by veritable spots. It probably would provide a valuable insight into Lope's writing process to classify the changes as far as possible.

The critical apparatus is arranged below the text on two levels: first a detailed description of the text, analyzing the writing process which led to changes in the text, indicating how passages were marked for omission, and noting minor details. The second level lists the variants in selected printed texts. The autograph of *El primero Benavides* contains 163 lines more than the *princeps* (Madrid, 1609). Since we are fortunate to have the original, we found it unnecessary to collate the text as it appears in the other seven located editions of the *Segunda parte*. Nor have we consulted a manuscript copy in an eighteenth-century hand preserved in the Library of the University of Seville. The variants listed are limited to those of the *princeps* and the two modern editions most currently in use, the Academy edition and the selection of Lope plays published by Aguilar (Madrid, 1955).

The Introduction ought to study the play as a whole and ought to deal with the following matters: bibliography, date of composition, structural analysis and versification, sources, and final evaluation. I already have discussed bibliography in my remarks on the editor and his text. The date of composition is given on the autographs themselves: for *El primero Benavides*, *"En Madrid a 15 de junio de 1600, Lope de Vega Carpio;"* for *Carlos V en Francia*, *"En Toledo, a 20 de noviembre de 1604, Lope de Vega Carpio."* The first edition of *El embuste* appeared in 1653, nine years after Vélez' death. I arrived at the date of 1617-18 by circumstantial evidence: (a) certain contacts with the works by Cervantes published in 1615, (b) similarities to other Vélez plays of the same period, and (c) the versification of *El embuste* compared with that of plays by Lope and Guillén de Castro composed between 1615 and 1620. Next, the editor should not simply retell the plot but should provide a structural analysis of the play, guided by changing verse forms. In 1609 Lope made some sweeping statements about the employ of the most frequent metres, statements which, although confirmed by modern editors and students, do not cover the metres' entire functional range. In general one can only say that a change of metre, most of the time but certainly not always, indicates a change in mood and atmosphere. In many editions, however, the analysis of versification is no more than a routine appendix of the Introduction. As for sources, the search clearly varies from play to play. In *El embuste* there are some episodes definitely borrowed from Cervantes, but beyond that there are no specific "sources." There are only motives. The principal motive is magic as practised by the servant Merlín, the main mover of the action. The theme of the play is the conflict between love and honor, certainly a most traditional and conventional theme in the *comedia*. But it is treated almost farcically. In *Carlos V en Francia* there are historical works which Lope demonstrably used. I had to reconstruct for Act I the historical background of the meeting in Nice in 1538 between the archrivals Charles V and Francis I of France, with Pope Paul III as the intermediary; the political events of the Cortes of Toledo of 1538 for Act II; and the splendid ceremonial entry of the Emperor into Paris in 1540 for Act III. In *El primero Benavides* we had to investigate the history of the kingdom of León around the year 1000. We tried to answer the question of what motivated Lope to write a genealogical play in 1600 about the origin of the Benavides family. We did not find any specific answer beyond the general observation that Lope wrote other genealogical plays with the action taking place at the beginning of Spanish history, an age of military prowess in the struggle against the Moors, with violent power struggles among the leading nobles on the one hand, and rural simplicity and monarchical devotion on the other hand. Lope glorified the heroic age of Spanish history. He emerged as a relatively faithful recorder of history in both plays: always, of course, as the dramatic poet he was, subordinating historical facts to his dramatic and patriotic art. Thus in *El primero Benavides* he placed the action of the play at the time of the boy king Alfonso V, crowned in 999, whose life is saved by the protagonist Sancho, the first Benavides. Actually, the "first Benavides" would have lived during the reign of Alfonso VII, Emperor of Castile and León (1105-50).

I am quite aware of the fact that source study *per se* is not literary criticism. But the relationship between the raw material of the sources and the finished work is an important contribution to that fundamental question of our profession: how reality is transformed into art.

Finally, a word about aesthetic evaluation, answering

the question, "Is the play good, bad or indifferent? " and "Why is it as it is?" Value judgment is a problem. If we ask questions about plot development from scene to scene, or from act to act, or about the motivation provided for the characters, we bring analytical points of view to bear on the play which we (or my generation at least) have been taught to ask in high school. These are useful and practical questions and may reveal the true nature of the play. In the case of *Carlos V* it turns out that the play is episodic, each act having its own story and existence. Unity is provided by the protagonist, who appears in all three acts. As for characterization: Carlos V is all imperial dignity and is endowed with a steadfast moral fibre resisting sexual temptation. Pacheco is of the *miles gloriosus* type. Fernandillo is a girl disguised as a man in pursuit of her lover who refuses to marry her. The Emperor, upholding the laws of the land, sees to it that the lover does marry her. She is also a type: *la mujer vestida de hombre* ("woman dressed as a man"). The most interesting and original character is Leonor, *dama*, who is really a mental case. She is obsessed by love for Charles V and offers herself to him body and soul. Each of these characters pursues his or her goal so that several strains of subplot are winding their way through this *comedia*. Is it a good play? I do not know, but I think I understand it, and I like it.

The content and the extent of the Notes is a matter for the editor to decide. As a rule of thumb one might say that whatever the trained editor does not understand, or does not know, needs explanation, be it a name (mythological or historical, or a place name), a word not in use today in modern Spanish, a very specialized term of a craft, or of a piece of clothing, etc., a grammatical or morphological phenomenon different from what is found in modern Spanish, a complex syntactical construction, or some rhetorical device such as anaphora, alliteration, and chiasmus. The explanation and clarification of imagery and its symbolism, if any, is an open field. How much the editor should provide depends very much on his own response to it, that is, on his own knowledge and sensitivity. However, in annotating we have to avoid the pitfalls of overdoing it and of pedantry.

In our two countries, a model of editing and annotation was created by the late professors John M. Hill and Mabel Margaret Harlan in their volume *Cuatro Comedias* (New York, 1941), editing one play each of the four prominent dramatists, Lope, Alarcón, Tirso de Molina, and Calderón. This is the text through which I learned the ropes. To their memory and that of their pupil, my teacher Claude E. Anibal, I dedicate this contribution.

INACCURACY AND CASTIGATION:
THE LESSSONS OF ERROR

Arthur Freeman

The textual shortcomings of the first collected edition of
Thomas Kyd, put forward by F.S. Boas in 1901 as an
Oxford English Text, are well enough known not to
require my harping on them. But out of curiosity, simply
to know how bad or undependable the rendering might
be, I chose almost at random two consecutive scenes from
Solyman and Perseda, a play attributed to Kyd, and did a
bit of malicious accounting. Now the first extant quarto
of *Solyman and Perseda* is undated, but almost certainly
appeared in 1592, during Kyd's lifetime, and only one
exemplar of this, what Malone calls "the authentick copy"
for the play, survives. It is probably (at least in one sheet)
an early one, for there is a mistake in lineation which a
paginary reprint of 1599 sets right, and I think we must
posit a lost later state of the first printing to explain the
subsequent correction. But save for this single confusion
the first quarto is our only authority for the text of
Solyman and Perseda, and as there is only one copy of it
the task of providing a modern text in old spelling would
seem to entail little more than transcribing the old text
letter by letter for its new compositor and reading one's
proofs. I might add that the second quarto need not even
contribute spelling variants, and that a type-facsimile of
about 1808 and the first nominally modern edition (1773,
based on the second quarto) are obviously of no present-
day textual relevance. But despite the simplicity of the
task, in the two scenes chosen, totalling 351 lines, Boas

commits no fewer than forty-four substantial errors, errors of spelling, line-division, capitalization, font-choice, citation of texts, and one unambiguous conjunction got wrong. I am not counting "false pointing" at all, which is Boas's own, nor his celebrated mistaking of the nineteenth-century facsimile for its 1599 original—to the end that its so-called "readings" are sometimes incorporated in the main text or notes; I count only the unsignalled variation from the simple and singular copy, when there is every evidence of plain error at the point of transcription.

Boas's text was reissued fifty-four years after its first appearance, lithographically reprinted "from corrected sheets of the first edition," but despite an abundant backlog of corrective evidence, the *text* of all the works was in no instance changed; so that the forty-four errors I noted remain comfortably in place. In 1959, however, an American Ph.D. thesis offered a new text of *Solyman and Perseda*—and only of the one play. That dissertation remains unpublished, save by xerography, and it is perhaps not fair therefore to tax it as if it were in print, but since the writer does permit himself some very caustic reflections upon Boas's technical accuracy, it may I think be pointed out that in the same 351 lines he, coming after the apparent botch, has made no fewer than fifty-two substantive errors of his own, including errors in spelling, a whole line omitted, and letters and words reversed—all this while supposedly following one copy-text and one only, having no modern printer to blame, and luxuriating in the accumulated scholarship and bibliographical advance of nearly sixty years, for what it was worth.

I will have my own chance to take my place in what seems now a history of progressive corruption for these poor lines, but until I am finished re-editing Kyd's works, hoping as usual to make no mistakes at all, I can only give earnest of my capacity for inaccuracy with a last statistic. A bibliographical article of 1969 by me on the printing of *The Spanish Tragedy*, which incidentally touches on the printing of *Solyman*, contains, in its thirteen pages of literal description, data, formulae and tables, at least ninety-two mistakes. I was shown them by a persistent and generous colleague about five years ago, and neither of us has any intention of correcting them just yet. For—and to this I shall want to return—in the long run not one of my conclusions is materially affected one way or the other by the errors, or by the corrections. Whether the article is worth anybody's revision I am not willing to guess.

But I am not reciting these appalling figures simply to be outrageous or outraged; I want to consider several aspects, some implicit in the figures, of literal or mechanical inaccuracy and minor error in the editing or reproduction of texts—any texts, really, but for our purposes and within my experience principally texts of early English drama. I mean the causes, physical and psychological, of small mistakes, the cures for them, the use of ulterior correction and the interaction of editor and castigator, the ultimate worth of the whole investigation and the instruction available from the process itself, and what attitudes toward text and scholarship can be assumed or extenuated from our success and failure at confronting inaccuracy. And I will want eventually to come home to a few practical suggestions which I hope are generally constructive, or at least specific enough to provoke practical response.

I: CUP TO LIP

Any new text may be regarded as the sum of the texts which actually precede it, from the chosen original copy or copies through all intermediate versions, whether physically expressed as drafts or printings or implicit only in the mind and behavior of those who produce the text. And in the production of the final text it is the mechanical process of transmission from (say) a unique sixteenth-century quarto largely in black letter to two thousand cloth-bound nine-point-Caslon equivalents which offers us our mechanical challenges, in a variety of ways and at any number of stages. Omitting from consideration, for the moment, the inferred processes leading up to our principal copy-text, we can trace the following main periods of transmission: (1) copy *via* editor to new printer's copy; (2) new printer's copy *via* compositor to type, and *via* printer to proof; (3) proof *via* correcting editor and correcting compositor to altered type, and *via* printer to revised proofs; (4) any number of repetitions of (3); (5) finally altered type *via* printer to pages. We shall want later to consider the treatment of those "final" pages by castigators quite after the fact of production, and the mechanics of subsequent revisal, but we begin by looking for potential causes of breakdown in the earlier action.

Obviously, as Clifford Leech[1] among others has observed, the practical business of turning out the new printer's copy almost always requires an editor to do some literal copying. And we should of course like to minimize this, in order to minimize the opportunity to corrupt— rather the opposite of what we might expect to want with original work. We begin frequently with a photograph or xerox, and at once a technical quarrel begins. But we *are* often obliged to make use of a film or photographic print if only to reduce wear and tear on a fragile original; and I do think it extremely dangerous, although I know many will disagree, to encourage untold generations of editors to go on working all through their labors with unique or very rare books and manuscripts (unique by definition) which

[1] "On Editing One's First Play," *Studies in Bibliography*, XXIII (1970), 61-70.

have been successfully reproduced in some kind of facsimile. When a Hinman collation of the unique undated original of *The Spanish Tragedy* with its 1969 Scolar Press facsimile reveals no blurs, I cannot myself justify using the pored-over quarto until the time comes for a last definitive check, and this especially since several editors in recent years have worked that book into a less-than-relaxed posture within its Panizzi morocco.

But photography has gained rather a bad reputation in editorial circles from even before W.W. Greg's famous review of the play facsimiles issued by John S. Farmer early in this century.[2] We must worry about distortion of line, unanimity of color, lack of paper-texture, and the ubiquitous fly-specks or dust on the lens masquerading as ink. We must indeed consult and always be ready to compare the originals. But *not* using photography is demonstrably more dangerous than using it, I think, as Greg himself seems to have revealed by the rare but explicable errors in his Malone Society Reprints, arising from his practice of copying out the original text by hand.[3] And in the instances when photography itself can serve to provide a text there is seldom any reason to dismiss it, or in fact to duplicate its function, as we can see in the frequently lamentable juxtaposition of facsimile and transcript in many descriptive bibliographies (e.g., Sir Geoffrey Keynes's Petty, Donne, and Evelyn). We should be aware of potential error in our photographic draft of the original copy, but never thus be wholly unwilling to benefit by it.

Unfortunately few modern compositors want to set, or are really capable of setting, from photographs of a text in unfamiliar fonts, or worse, from hand-corrected photo-

[2]"Mr. Farmer's Facsimiles," *The Athenaeum,* no. 4455 (1913), 316.

[3]I have this by hearsay, several years ago, but from the late John Crow; certainly the two mistakes in the reprint of *The Spanish Tragedy* (1602) look like mistranscriptions.

graphs. It is nearly always an editor's task to render as new printer's copy something legibly written or typed, with the normative alterations of script "s" 's, "u" and "v," and so forth, ligatures eliminated (although often to be resupplied in different patterns by the new printer), and so from film or plate or xerox a fresh stage of text intervenes, and offers its own occasions for corruption. Handwritten transcripts of either photograph or original are probably quite unusual now, although some must crop up to account for special blunders, and thus caution us about errors to expect. Boas must have copied Kyd's *Verses of Praise and Joy* by hand, if we are to explain a serious misreading, from a unique source, in one line:

> The Pope, to prop his minions state
> doth golden proffers make . . . .

"Minions," which becomes an operative part of at least one rhetorical analysis of Kyd, and of course figures in the Kyd concordance and in all arguments for authorship derived from it, is in fact "ruinous" in the original—from which we can, I think, deduce some characteristics of Boas's own running hand. Direct typewriting has more or less supplanted manuscript for most of us, I assume, and no doubt future analyses of errors will find, as I have already in twice-typed students' papers, mechanical errors of a deceptive plausibility derived from correctape, leaps in manual or electric spacing, loose golfballs, worn matrices (especially h/n), and letters adjacent on the keyboard. Textual scholars have already learned to deal with the reconstructed eccentricities of the typewriter in general; soon, no doubt, we shall be able to posit the make of a writer's machine inferentially, and to draw new textual implications from our knowledge. I knew a poet in the early 'fifties who was drawn to emulate e. e. cummings' lower-case mannerisms by a faulty shift key on his own machine, although a new one did not change his ways.

Another stage of the transmitted text, perhaps dividing original or facsimile from typed new printer's copy, is very frequently a mocked-up set of a prior and perhaps unsatisfactory printed edition of the same. We adopt these generally for the sake of convenience only, providing as they do versions of the text in modern fonts, perhaps with new pointing and spelling—at least enough redesigned to make it easy for us to redesign or correct or alter in turn. These crypto-intermediate texts can cause all manner of mechanical error, of course, although in the long run they probably reduce it; the hazard is always that we will hypnotically follow a plausible misprint or misreading, and the attendant embarrassment (as with Bowers' recent Cambridge Marlowe) may be disproportionate to the effective plagiary. Surely if we continue to use this sort of aid we should at least refrain from the most extreme reflections on our immediately prior text, and if we must damn it, we might also say what we are doing.

Most if not all the processes of transmission mentioned above, between original copy-text and new printer's copy, involve more than physical action, however, and one must confront the psychological factors influencing small error as well. In the time between inscriptions that a word or character is lodged in the editor's mind it is subject to affections far less easily determined or corrected than the physical hazards we know. And this becomes increasingly relevant as the complexity of the copy-text itself increases, when alternative readings must be suspended even momentarily in the discriminator's short-term memory.

Expectable spellings and sequential expressions cause trouble here: unless we realize an eccentricity may occur, we are almost bound mentally to correct what we see in our copy—as the Bodleian Malone exhibition catalogue made him Edmund, not Edmond (by no means an uncommon slip), or as Josuah Sylvester inevitably turns up Joshua. And our editors' silent editors, the typesetters, may be counted on from time to time for an *un-Hamlet*, for *The White Devil*, or for Jane Austen's *Love and Friendship*, generally, if not always, because the odd words or spellings look like simple transpositions or mechanical lapses. As the editor subsequently checks his proof, in the second stage of textual transmission, he will often have to restore again, if he got it right once, a *lectio difficilior* when the simpler has obstinately reintruded. A technique here to be considered is red-pencilling such readings, in the retained duplicate new printer's copy, as are most likely to become altered through somebody else's unfamiliarity with them; another is to bring in a fresh pair of eyes—and would that we had them! Perhaps a pool or exchange, like a dating bank, for trading off the tasks of proofreading, at some stage in the correction, might be established.

Modernization of spelling and punctuation probably gives rise to less obvious mistakes than do the Anglo-American discrepant conventions. I do not know how many anglicized spellings or pointings are to be found in my Signet edition of *Henry VI Part II*, owing to the fact (I am now confessing) that I worked with a mock-up of John Dover Wilson's Cambridge text, but I do know that my excellent general editor caught several. Some trouble may lie here in the frequency with which we all adjust our reading and writing by turns to English or American rules, and it may be exacerbated by occasional inclinations of Elizabethan orthography toward the modern American style (e.g., in -or endings). But this is not strictly relevant to the more conservative old-spelling texts I am primarily considering.

A more interesting kind of mental error is the adoption

of a particularly dreadful misreading, often (the blackmail of post-Freudian thought forces me to assume) through fear or guilt or self-loathing. If the catastrophic boner in the 1631 "Wicked" Bible seventh commandment ("Thou shalt commit adultery") was indeed no more than an accident, it was punished as a crime, with no consideration of *mens sua*. And while possibly here sabotage was to blame in the dropping of the one critical particle,[4] it is difficult not to suspect something more subconscious in the 1651 Corinthians reading, "that the unrighteous shall inherit the Kingdom of God."[5] Most of us can remember similarly revealing slips with amusement or chagrin; surely in even the most subdued dislexia there lurks a compulsion to misspell, misquote, or misrepresent the authoritative precedent in an especially garish way. Here again only proofreading in the word-as-object manner, or the exchange of responsibilities, is likely to prove efficient, for if once we were blinded by our own hidden desire to misread, we will probably be so blinded twice.

The howler, or "glaring error," may also arise from a concealed wish to outrage, I suppose, but it seems to owe some of its frequency simply to typographical variation. As newspaper headlines seem especially vulnerable, so are titles, initial words in capitals or large fonts, captions, running heads even in skeletons, and characters in display or in isolation. One wonders how the publisher John Smethwick permitted his elegant 1619 folio of Drayton's *Works* to be issued spelling his own name "Swethwick," and who set it so; how Spenser came to be "Edward" on the title of Chalkhill's *Thealma and Clearchus*, or Allen

---

[4]Cf. A.S. Herbert, ed., T.H. Darlow and H.F. Moule, *Historical Catalogue of Printed Editions of the English Bible, 1525-1961* (London and New York, 1962), p. 162. A German Bible of 1731, not seen by Herbert, is supposed to contain the same error.

[5]This is however a notoriously ill-printed duodecimo Bible.

Tate to be "Alan" in Hart Crane's *White Buildings*; or the dates of *Humphrey Clinker*, Caxton's Gower, the Oxford Rufinus,[6] the "1719" English Perrault and the "1353" Tonson *Pharsalia*[7] to be so comically bobbled. The cause of many such titular errors may be partly that large words are too obviously "visible" to be quite *read*, and partly that the writer rarely sees anything like early proof of such matter (titles, copyright data, colophons, spine-labels, etc.); the cure may be simply to set aside a special inspection of all exceptional print in one's last proofs, treating this portion of the text as separate from the main body; one's eye stays sharper if it need not constantly adjust to changing type-sizes, or leap over typographically unoccupied blank space.

II: Not Talking Shop

Going on to the hazards of the second, third, and fourth stages of textual transmission, we encounter above all the relationship of editor and printers, about which unfortunately few editors seem to know or care a great deal; and ignorance of just what may happen after the submission of a clean new printer's copy to the press itself or to the publisher can easily result in a botch as celebrated as the Yale facsimile of the First Folio. The physical appearance of our new printer's copy should concern us, for while some English compositors are still reasonably willing and able to cope with abominable (if native) handwriting, and with typescript heavily corrected in manuscript, or even to set

[6]Cf. Madan, I, 250, for other misdated early English books.

[7]Especially cited by Jacob Blanck, *The Title-Page as Bibliographical Evidence* (Berkeley, 1966), p. 5. The full imprint of this pamphlet is "School of Librarianship / University of California. Berkeley / 1966," and it should be noted that Blanck was not shown proof of his own title-page. The task of seeing that through the press was undertaken by the Dean of the School.

from negative photostats, [8] most American compositors will not cope with these, and probably ought not to make the attempt. Providing a very clean new printer's copy can of course cost us one or more extra intermediate drafts, which we don't want; some kind of compromise between the confusingly sloppy and the deceptively handsome has to be settled on between editors and printers, and it should be settled specifically as close to the former as is mutually acceptable. And though it should hardly require mentioning, the editor must of course retain a copy, in this instance certainly a photograph or xerox, of the finally submitted new printer's copy. Lamentably many of us seem to rely on the penultimate draft as a substitute; I wonder if less than a quarter of the time some part of the submitted copy will not get lost or damaged during the process of production.

A delicate matter is that of the estimate, by the editors, of the intelligence and capability of the compositors, because the extent and detail of supplementary special instructions for setting depends on this, likewise any relegation of corrective responsibility. One does not really want to be edited at the press, but one does want to be at least advised if something seems wrong or odd to the last house-proofreader or compositor. [9] To this end some kind of preliminary explanation, in writing, would often be useful, though one may risk seeming officious, offensive, and hopelessly naïve in listing self-evident cautions for an experienced worker at the press. But taking too much for granted can be quite disastrous: an issue of a distinguished journal recently was virtually copy-read by pro-

---

[8] I have seen such working copy employed as late as the 1950s by the Nonesuch Press for John Hayward.

[9] A poem of my own, "Expatriate's Return," passed through two printings as "Expatriot's Return" because each publisher thought I was making a pun; I was not.

fessional printers, with the result that in three poems by a most eminent American poet there are two testimonies to his own inability to spell; the original typescript indeed had more. In one of the errors[10] the printers would have been presumptuous to have judged an apparent archaism or variant as a mistake—although it was. The very best thing, if we can manage it, is to meet the printers in person (whatever they say) and to become at least slightly familiar with their experience, methodology, and facilities. We spend so much time trying to measure such skills and habits in sixteenth- and seventeenth-century printers that it seems ludicrous not to put any substantial effort into understanding the work of our own. And knowing at least whether we are being set in linotype, as usual in America, or monotype, commoner in England, is quite essential, for certain kinds of error are virtually impossible in the former but frequent in the latter, even after revises;[11] film composition, especially *via* the dreaded computer, offers other assets and risks. We need to know how these processes work, and how they can forestall, abet, or thwart us in our revisions. An example of the kind of technical problem, for example, which is proper only to the printing stage of transmission (and that by monotype chiefly) is the breakage or slippage or wearing of type, with resulting differences between proof and final print. Ordinarily a house copy-editor signals the worn or tilted characters, but we too should be aware of the potential erosion of points (e.g., comma from semicolon) and letters, and we should never regard an area of text altogether "safe" simply because one proof-pull has seemed perfect.

Proofreading itself has been discussed often and well

---

[10]They are "Potomic" for Potomac, and "enterprize."

[11] I have especially in mind the reversal or scrambling of thin types at the end of a line (e.g., "I,") which fall down.

enough to be skimped here. I do think that most writers and editors tend to read too much proof without resting, though, and that generally too little time is allowed by publishers for the task. If we are to read letter-by-letter backwards and from the foot of the galley up we had better use two sets of proof and actually cross off or underline the characters as we find them true, and we had better not keep at this for hours without pause. I think the use of fresh readers is an excellent idea, if it can be done short of coercing one's spouse or student, and might best be achieved by exchanging second readings with the editor of another text; but at all events the proper editor should himself do both the initial and the final proofing. And these cautions will be profitable at each stage of revisal, no matter how often the printers are willing to adjust the type and return new proofs.

There are two very special nightmares of the print-shop, one of which with luck may never affect us. But undeclared resetting is unfortunately relatively common. A crushed letter in a block of linotype will result in a whole paragraph being recast, just as a proof-correction would have, and if this occurs late in the day the printers may well do it on their own and say nothing. In monotype a pied line, page, or even sheet could be treated similarly. All we can do is beg the pressmen to tell us about each accident, even if it means some kind of commercial understanding between us and publisher and shop, which short of personal guarantee or sponsorship may be unprecedented. This is indeed an area of risk where a great deal of improvement or insurance could be forthcoming—had we the means.

Out-and-out sabotage at the shop is, I hope, a rare event. The worst modern example known to me was a methodical reversal of data and other quite deceptive alterations of evidence and judgement in one of the large volumes of the *Bibliography of American Literature*. These deliberate corruptions appear almost certainly to have been the work of some printers with a grievance against their press, put in during the complex stages of final proofing; only good luck caught the issue, and rereading an entire volume of proof delayed publication no less than a year. The distress of the author, whose intentions and achievement were so recklessly aborted, can scarcely be estimated.

A special set of caveats should be registered for editors— or indeed "presenters"—of modern reprint series, those produced from photographs or originals with or without introductions or even collations and identification of copy-text. Most reprint publishers want, from their editors, nothing but instructions about what to photograph, and copy for the preliminary matter; proofs of the latter come predictably back, but only the most obdurate editor can persuade the most compliant of publishers to show him proofs of the final main text. This is because, as I am told, once plates have been made from photographs, the cost of altering them is prohibitive; so perhaps we should insist, or try to insist, on a look at the film before plate-making. In the first such series I edited I was politely but firmly denied access either to film or to proof of my texts, and uneasily settled for a long emphatic list of instructions from me to the printers. And indeed the printers were careful not to mask out foxing or fly-specks, as I had begged; but I had not thought it necessary to explain the need of preserving catchwords and signatures. The results were almost comic, especially in one volume whose bibliographical preface is largely devoted to analysis of the odd but revealing signing of the sheets, no vestige of which remains in the reprint.[12] The publishers (Garland

[12]This is the Frank Cass reprint of W.H. Ireland, *Vortigern and Henry II* (London, 1971); other volumes in the series *Eighteenth Century Shakespeare* are similarly defective. Cf. Richard Proudfoot in *Shakespeare Survey*, XXIV (1971), 171.

Press) of the present volume were far more obliging in another such series, but I fear that the long and labored prefatory discussion of variant settings in one important volume is about vitiated by the absence of the promised variants; they were never photographed and nobody checked.[13] The real troubles with these series are that they are generally too big, too commercially constrained, produced too quickly, and overseen either by knowledgeable editors who don't yet know their editorial rights or by old hands who don't really care. In the wake of the mismanaged Readex pre-Restoration drama-on-microfiche and many other such reprints from copy chosen almost at random, one can only tremble at the announced project (Boni/Readex) to reproduce the whole substance of the *B.A.L.* on microfilm.

When the plates are locked up—if monotype—for the last time, and pass the last proofing,[14] and the real sheets roll off them, we hope, of course, although we are taught never to expect it, for something close to perfection, something almost error-free. And if we have performed our tasks faithfully and have had help at the press, we do have a right to hope. But for how much? For more, surely, than in the texts of Kyd I began by checking; for less, probably, than in the Foulis Press "immaculate Horace," or in the new Oxford Bible. For the disclosure of an error in the latter the Clarendon Press long offered a guinea, "but," says the 1922 retrospective account, "very few guineas have been earned."[15] Here we have a fine incentive, and

[13]Francis Meres, *Palladis Tamia* (rpt. New York, 1974), in the Garland Press series *The English Stage: Attack and Defence.*

[14]Here a specialist house proofreader with an understanding of last-stage hazards is especially to be desired: Stinehour Press, of Vermont, has traditionally been very good at this.

[15]*Some Account of the Oxford University Press, 1468-1921* (Oxford, 1922), p. 59.

a potentially immense population of independent proof-readers with no end of time; it would be a most interesting if eccentric use of foundation money—say no more than a few hundred dollars a volume—so to "cover" any new standard text. One could offer some cash or book-credit per correction, unless earlier caught, and nominal recognition in an errata bulletin to be published a year or more after the text. And the benefit of the exercise for the generalized proofreading eye would be not inconsiderable.[16]

III: Afterwords

Given at last the machining and issue of our text, the labors of the first editor performed and canonized, the pursuit of accuracy now enters a new and more public stage. Critic, reviewer, or castigator (including of course the self-castigator as he rereads his own work) begin a collaboration with the text's editor which is rarely altogether kindly, but which if properly observed and employed is of obvious importance. We are trying to perfect; we need help; and though the gratitude we normally feel for the previous reader who has corrected the index or ticked off misprints in our copy of a book may be attenuated when the book is our own, that special relationship between the establisher and the examiner should never be lost in the asperities of critical conduct, or in personal sensitivities. Historically, to be sure, the record is uneven, and the "collaboration" often resembles pitched battle. We think of the eighteenth century, we think of Theobald and Pope, Edwards or Heath and Warburton,

---

[16]An interesting attempt to calculate the probable limits of correction, with some astute observations on the treatment of proof, is in "The Calculus of Error, or Reflections on Editing Hooker," a paper for the December 1975 R.E.T.S. conference by W. Speed Hill. He has kindly allowed me to read it before its presentation.

Kenrick and Johnson, Ritson and Steevens and latterly
Malone, none of these relationships much tainted with
amity. But the interaction was rarely unproductive. Theobald in *Shakespeare Restored* (1726) offered approximately 102 emendations, corrections, or groups of corrections to Pope's text of *Hamlet*.[17] Of these I should call
sixteen non-substantive, two substantive but very minor,
thirty-five wrong or at least dubious, and forty-nine
probably right; only three of the latter are corrections of
misprints, and two call attention to deliberate bowdleriza-
tion—with which Theobald however declares he agrees in
spirit. Still, over half right is an admirable proportion,
especially when we consider that Theobald almost certainly employed fewer, not more, old texts than Pope,
and in fact clearly did *not* use any of the only three
authoritative texts, i.e., the first and second quartos, and
the first folio.[18] But thirty-five faulty corrections is rather
an alarming quantity, even if Theobald himself scrapped
many of the most eccentric ones in his own 1733 edition.
Pope's use of Theobald's corrections in his second edition
of 1728, though played down by him in his prefatory
acknowledgements, was considerable, of course, and so
was Theobald's use of the 1728 Pope in both 1733 and
1740; so that in spite of the acrimony, *The Dunciad*, and
the contest of editorial principles, the text of Shakespeare
benefited from the quarrel. What indeed offended most of
the Shakespearean establishment of the century about
Theobald—Warburton, Hanmer, and Johnson among
others—was not his rationale or results but his manners,

---

[17]"Approximately" because Theobald lumps together many of his suggestions, especially those for repunctuating speeches.

[18]No copy of the first quarto was then known, but Theobald's main
authorities were the 1637 quarto, the second folio, and a quarto edited by
"the accurate Mr. [John] Hughs." The last Furness (New Variorum edition)
suggests was Theobald's fabrication, but it is indeed an acting edition of 1718.

and despite what many of the more Tory editors said about Theobald, they rarely failed to adopt his most plausible readings on any personal grounds.

Thomas Edwards' amusing and popular teasing of Warburton is less directed at inaccuracy than at presumption and needless emendation, but as a castigator he too contributes to a more "refined" old-style text; yet here and with Heath, Kenrick, Holt, and even the positive John Monck Mason on Steevens we are more in the realm of judgemental critique than of simple or literal reform. Joseph Ritson, however, is a nit-picker almost without parallel, whose extraordinary sharpness is at least equalled by his extraordinary vituperation. Having bitterly assaulted an appropriately sardonic rival in George Steevens during the 'eighties, in 1792 he turned his captious attentions to a more temperate and more formidable antagonist, Edmond Malone. This episode of editorial construction (i.e., the 1790 variorum), castigation *(Cursory Criticisms of . . . Malone*, 1792) and response (*A Letter to the Rev. Richard Farmer, D.D.*, 1792) is instructive. For the 1790 text of Shakespeare is remarkably good,[19] and rarely controversial; Ritson's corrections are few, but mainly valid; and Malone's own treatment of his Zoilist adversary is exemplary both for spirit and for tact. In over 100,000 lines, says Malone, containing 1654 "emendations" of earlier editions, Ritson discovered no more than thirteen errors, five of which Malone can dispute. Like Pope, and with a touch of Pope's mock-graciousness, he accepts the eight remaining corrections "with gratitude." The victory of wit is easily Malone's, though a modern reader cannot help but pause over his obvious misrepresentation

---

[19] For simple literal accuracy within the limits of its own definition, the best eighteenth-century edition of all is I believe Capell's.

of the very extent of Ritson's examination: for the corrections are confined to the first volumes only, out of ten, and do not begin to involve 100,000 lines. Need Malone have misled us?

Further to illuminate the curious symbiosis here of text-giver and taker-away is the open, essentially "oral" style of Malone's self-defence, and the anality of Ritson's curt rhetoric, which depends largely on deliberate misreading and mean jibes, crude sarcasm, and an animus which transparently betrays jealousy and possessive rage. One almost pathetic token of the castigator's frustration is his prospectus for an ambitious new Shakespeare edition—one rather beyond Ritson's means, and never to be more than begun—as the ultimate corrective to the announced new Malone-in-quarto—which ironically was abortive as well. But in spite of the lugubrious personal involvements here, Ritson, as with the Irelands and the *Vortigern* controversy, has uses which transcend the sensational and the few scraps of correction he offers. Malone was driven to defend himself in terms revealing both to us, and, one may think, to himself, by codifying his practice and clarifying his method and intent, I believe as well as it has ever been done, in the pages of his *Letter to Farmer.* So the relationship of critic and criticized, turned back on itself, yields more than the few gains in mechanical accuracy; moreover, as perhaps the least attractive of all eighteenth-century exchanges for rudeness and malice, it gives us something to consider in formulating an ideal pattern of the correcting relationship, a kind of ethics of critique. This may not extend beyond suggesting mildness or humility in the corrector, when the editor himself has not behaved badly, but even that would be helpful. The mirror, in Ritson, of arrogance, nonproductivity, and nonetheless correctness, in Malone of industry, openness both to error and to mending it, and arrogance again, but of a more acceptable and justifiable breadth, and, in their matching-up, of an ugly but spirited and at last beneficial test, is one I think representative of the extreme interaction of editorial work and review. Since 1792 the emulators of Ritson for spleen have been with us unfortunately more often than those of Malone for comparative magnanimity. But I suppose that is a natural result of specialization and the narrowing proprietorship of the past.

Castigation, which can easily become an end in itself, and (like criticism) attain a certain attractiveness independent of its subject, does still require that subject, much as the subject requires correction—or for that matter an editor requires something to edit. Coming next in line is really a lucky accident, and we all have to be grateful even to our most slipshod precursors who have set us our tasks and made possible or necessary our achievement. As the editor may have benefited from a mocked-up text of any maligned predecessor, so may he grudgingly appreciate the sharp-eyed discoveries of his own after-lookers, although like the embattled writer challenging his critics to write anything but criticism he may understandably resent the castigator who, like Ritson, cannot subsequently rise to the risk of putting forth his own editorial adventures for review or rebuke.

IV: "The other is a horse still."

"Counsels of imperfection," as they appear in Samuel Butler's serenely skeptical notebooks, lead us to learn what we can from every species of mistake. What lessons from editorial error, large and small? It is true that a clever specialist can learn a good deal about undeclared procedure from the analysis of a flaw or blunder, as we know something about Boas's manuscript copying from "minions" and something about a jacket-writer's hand

from the English Penguin's linking up F. Scott Fitzgerald
and "the 1933 age."[20] In earlier texts we find evidence of
typesetting practice, by dictation, from variously defective
copy in various sequences; as the odd moveable line in
Solyman and Perseda told us, evidence of lost states,
issues, or editions of our text; and all manner of useful or
useless evidence about compositors' predilections, learning,
ignorance and equipment. But from the incidence of minor
error, the causes of it, and the treatment of it in our own
time we can learn something as well about its eventual
ubiquity and importance.

Everyone knows, or is supposed to know, that error of
some kind simply is always there, that the perfect text is
a chimera. Even if this is not strictly true, in fact and in
prospect, for some short texts are obviously pure, and
machines will no doubt come some day to eliminate most
of our small human mistakes, it is nonetheless a properly
chastening notion. But what therefore to *do* about it? We
can assault it with all guns—those obvious minor techniques, more money, and more time, even adding a few
ruthless exclusions simply to prevent or discourage preter-
naturally error-prone scholars from undertaking, alone,
editorial tasks, or certain well-meaning but historically
all-thumbs printers and publishers from taking responsibility for complicated texts. Arbitration would be
difficult, tendentious, and perhaps heartless, but the net
effect could hardly be more demoralizing than the proli-
feration of bad texts by momentarily fashionable editors
and houses.[21] Still, is the pursuit of accuracy really worth
this kind of worry and effort? For the sake of argument

---

[20]This compositorial scramble of "the jazz age" was a discovery of John
Crow's in a Penguin edition of *The Great Gatsby.*

[21]Especially pernicious are the anthologies to which any number of distinguished academic personalities put their names, while a less eminent colleague
generally prepares the copy.

and tentative conclusion I want to suggest that, at present, it is not.

Finally the intense search for the elimination of literal inaccuracy is after all very boring, as the substance of this very paper is boring and dry, and it well may exhaust energies otherwise best devoted to producing some kind of result, good or bad, but at least a result. As long as Malone fears Ritson we will have suspended editions of Greene, Middleton, Massinger and (I can testify) Kyd; Kyd languishes in part because I am lazy and in part because I became transfixed and then bored by the problems addressed here. Reckoning up particular trees over and over keeps us away from the real woods of an edition, complete with commentary and opinion, illustration and sympathetic presentation, and such achievements as F.L. Lucas' Webster or McKerrow's Nashe have been lost for other authors, not only to the poor Marston of H.H. Wood or the fine but still naked Bowers' Dekker, but also to the very absence of new annotated texts of any number of missed authors. Is the pursuit of perfection to blame? Just what edition of Shirley or Ford or Massinger or the Shakespeare Apocrypha[22] are we supposed these days to consult? And to go back to my own virtual culture of mistakes cited far above, should I spend whatever scholarly energy I have (to say nothing of a journal's available space) tidying up a sad article whose arithmetic is wrong but not misleading, when no conclusion derived from the faulty tables is affected, rather than go on to other immediate and potentially useful editorial efforts? Of course I should be tactful enough to keep quiet about past disas-

[22]Certainly not the new and appalling collection of *Shakespeare's Doubtful Plays*, the text of which is an unabashed reprint of the American reprint of the mid-nineteenth-century supplement to Halliwell-Phillipps. Presumably Tucker Brooke's edition is still under copyright control.

ters or no one will trust me in the future, but on occasion one must side with the Abbé Vertot: "mon siege," despite all your new evidence, "est fait;" let somebody else revise it.

I want to close with two practical suggestions. First, given the energy expended on present-day correction of editions in reviews, correspondence, and conversation, may we not have some kind of accountancy, delivered regularly and formally in one expectable place, of known queries, acknowledged mistakes, and corrigenda? Even if publishers will not offer errata years later, learned journals surely can,[23] and the altered reissues of texts (like Bowers' Dekker) or even studies (like mine of Kyd) which embody substantial correction should be cited or signalled whenever possible; otherwise the whole process of correction mocks itself.

Second, if we do regard, as everyone claims to regard, all prepared texts as somehow asymptotic to the chimerical true text, if no edition is ever going to be quite perfect, does this not lead us toward a less rigid faith in the whole process of amelioration than is generally expressed among us? Indeed if the old texts were never quite what the author had in mind, and the new ones not quite to our liking, is it not time to recognize the general limits of our expectations in getting everything right, and to concentrate on other aspects of the editorial responsibility? I worry about the narrowing of scope, of ambition, and achievement in formerly less fastidious scholars; when the palm is awarded to the product of computerized comparisons plugged into collational formulae, in effect the work of textual mechanics overseen only by the shadow of an editorial presenter, it is difficult to know whence

---

[23]*PBSA* may have stretched this notion with its addenda to *all* bibliographies (Montana imprints, etc.).

the wise commentary, the just evaluation, and the illuminating context or perspective are to come. Can we perhaps, in assuming a less reverent attitude toward accuracy, come some of us away from the despotism of pure text, and put in for a more democratic division of attention and accolade in editorial functions—not the least of which is getting some semblance of a job done?

In characterizing the witty strictures of Thomas Edwards on Bishop Warburton's imposing but wrongheaded Shakespeare, Dr. Johnson remarked, "A fly, Sir, may sting a stately horse and make him wince; but one is but an insect, and the other is a horse still."[24] It is unfortunate, if typical, of Johnson to have picked Warburton as his horse, since not many of us would greatly praise that edition, but as usual his critical application stands on its own. A horse *is* a horse still, and what even Warburton wanted to do was to establish a text, a full text, and a reader's text, and not to content himself with the raw material for one. Better editors produced and will produce better editions, and their gadflies are always necessary and not always as selfishly tormenting as the one in Johnson's figure. To be more and more accurate is the burden of my study, but I have to conclude apologetically, the stately animal my accuser. The last lesson of error, for me, is that we can err grossly in our zeal to mistake least.

[24]James Boswell, *The Life of Samuel Johnson*, ed. L.F. Powell and G.B. Hill, I (Oxford, 1934), 263 n.

Members of the Conference

Miriam M. Baum, *University of Cincinnati*
Thomas L. Berger, *St. Lawrence University*
W. F. Blissett, *University of Toronto*
Meriel Bradford, *Canada Council*
Marion E. Brown, *University of Toronto*
Roberta Buchanan, *Memorial University
of Newfoundland*
David Carnegie, *University of Otago, New Zealand*
Neil Carson, *University of Guelph*

Martin Cohen, *Concordia University*
Beatrice Corrigan, *University of Toronto*
J. A. Dainard, *University of Toronto*
Richard A. Davies, *Acadia University*
Hugo de Quehen, *University of Toronto*
Eric Domville, *University of Toronto*
Alvin I. Dust, *University of Waterloo*
David G. Esplin, *University of Toronto*
G. Blakemore Evans, *Harvard University*
Anthony J. Farrell, *St. Mary's University*
W. Craig Ferguson, *Queen's University*
Arthur Freeman, *London, England*
Barry Gaines, *University of Tennessee*

David Galloway, *University of New Brunswick*
Paul M. Gaudet, *University of Western Ontario*
Ellen S. Ginsberg, *The Catholic University of America*
Francess G. Halpenny, *University of Toronto*
G. A. Hamel, *University of Toronto*
Robert L. Hathaway, *Colgate University*
George R. Hibbard, *University of Waterloo*
F. David Hoeniger, *University of Toronto*
Henry D. Janzen, *University of Windsor*
Alexandra F. Johnston, *University of Toronto*
Joel H. Kaplan, *University of British Columbia*
Anne Lancashire, *University of Toronto*
Ian Lancashire, *University of Toronto*
Richard G. Landon, *University of Toronto*
Jill L. Levenson, *University of Toronto*
C. C. Love, *University of Toronto*
H. R. MacCallum, *University of Toronto*
John McClelland, *University of Toronto*
Warren T. McCready, *University of Toronto*
J. W. R. Meadowcroft, *Concordia University*
Mary E. Moeslein, *University of Toronto*
Caroline Monahan, *University of Victoria*
Ruth Mortimer, *Smith College*
Eugene F. Murphy, *Hobart and William Smith Colleges*
Desmond G. Neill, *University of Toronto*
J. H. Parker, *University of Toronto*
R. B. Parker, *University of Toronto*
G. R. Proudfoot, *King's College, University of London*
David Nicholas Ranson, *University of Akron*
Arnold G. Reichenberger, *University of Pennsylvania*
A. G. Rigg, *University of Toronto*

John M. Robson, *University of Toronto*

Peter Seary, *University of Toronto*

Anna Seary, *Toronto*

Raymond Shady, *University of Toronto*

G.B. Shand, *York University*

Michael J. Sidnell, *University of Toronto*

J. A. B. Somerset, *University of Western Ontario*

C. Alan Soons, *State University of New York, Buffalo*

Prudence Tracy, *University of Toronto Press*

Hermine J. van Nuis, *Indiana University–Purdue University at Fort Wayne*

Alan R. Young, *Acadia University*

INDEX